The
Blue Settee
a life made new

Susan Y Barnett

Copyright © 2012 Susan Y Barnett
All rights reserved.

ISBN-10: 1477587446
EAN-13: 978-1477587447

Dedication

For my wonderful grandchildren: Emmy, Abigail, Dominic and Hollie - my little gifts from heaven. It is truly a privilege to be your Granny.

Contents

What others are saying about The Blue Settee

Throughout the cancer and treatment, the one thing that I kept Susan going with, was the thought of our wedding, and the day she stood at my side to say our vows was the best day of my life. Neither of us had been a hundred per cent sure if she would make it, and there was a time when I wasn't even sure if I would be attending a funeral or a wedding at the end of her treatment. But I am happy to say, she did make it.

She's a very strong woman, and I knew if anyone was going to make it through cancer – Susan was! It was touch and go at times, and it was at those times that I would remind her of her beliefs as a Christian – to keep her going. It was important to keep her spirits up.

When she started to write this book, I knew it was something she had to do, and I have supported her with it because it has helped her to make sense of things. There were things that she found very difficult to write about and though I couldn't help her much with writing those things, I knew that without them being in the book, it wouldn't have been as honest or as real.

I am very proud of Susan for what she has achieved in writing this book and think it will really help people who might be going through a similar experience – either like me as a carer, or like Susan had been – facing serious illness.

Ron Barnett
Susan's husband

I've known Sue now for over ten years. Being married to Kelly, her eldest daughter, I have had a unique insight into the challenges Sue has had to deal with over the past few years. In that time, the transformation in Sue's life has been remarkable.

From the peaks of new grandchildren, through the valleys of critical illness, divorce and family estrangement, this book is a window into the life of a lady who found restoration and a better tomorrow.

Throughout the pages that follow you will laugh and cry, feel sympathy and share in moments of blissful happiness. This story is, however, about much more than Sue's battle with cancer. It is a living testament to the power of our incomparable Saviour to comfort and heal, to restore and set free. It is the chronicle of an ordinary woman, and an extraordinary God.

Adrian Turner
Susan's Son-in-law
Elder
Elim Pentecostal Church, West Bromwich

I'll never forget the night a few of us gathered with Susan to pray for her after her recent diagnosis of throat cancer. I knew that Susan at that point, whilst knowing that God loved her didn't really have the faith, the confidence that God could heal, she hadn't got it. In fact I believe that she only came that night because I had asked her, she'd come really out of obedience to what her church leader had suggested. That didn't worry me, that was what church family was there for.... to stand in the gap, to be the hedge that surrounds... to be that body that holds it together when one part is suffering and can't help itself. And that is simply what we did.

We were there when we were needed, we prayed, we supported, we loved, we believed. We were simply being what Jesus called us to be, fellow followers who show His love by the way we loved each other, people who took care of each other. What was truly incredible was witnessing how Susan's faith and trust began to grow and blossom. She was not only walking a dark path to recovery but alongside that, in all of the pain and suffering; somehow she was reconnecting in a new and significant way to her Saviour.

Susan's story whilst unique to her is a story that is unfolding day by day in many of our churches. What this book does is give Church Leaders and Christ followers a refreshing glimpse of what happens when faith collides with potential disaster. Susan's honest and sometimes very direct approach opens our eyes to some of the challenges, trials and fears that maybe someone you know is going through at the moment. It a story that although incredibly down to earth and truthful gives the reader hope, courage and the audacity to believe that our God is more than able.

Mark Bean - Now Church Leader

In tough times, there are two realities we need to face. Firstly, there are the facts. Secondly, there is the truth. Susan Barnett is an inspirational woman who had the courage to face the facts but more than that, dared to believe God's truth. Her story is as real as it gets.

Susan has experienced the adversity of illness and yet, despite everything she has gone through, has actually emerged all the better than ever before! Cancer didn't beat her...and she lives to tell the tale.

There was hope for Susan. There is HOPE for you! Reading this book will inspire you to believe. Go on....I dare you to believe!

Roy Todd, international speaker and author
www.roytodd.org

İntroduction to my Story

The 'Women of Destiny' team at my Church organised a ladies lunch with a visiting Speaker.

The invitation to all had me intrigued. I had attended other ladies' functions in the past at other churches and had enjoyed this time. So I bought my ticket with the usual expectations - that it would be a pleasant time, that it would be one which would have its customary blessings and at the same time ensuring that the women had time out from their busy lives.

As I entered the church I was greeted with the sight of a beautifully laid out room, with every detail attended to, including flowers and I felt as though I was being welcomed into an atmosphere of love and excitement.

As I sat at my table, I have to be honest; I was beginning to wish I hadn't attended. I was trying hard to be polite and to chat, but I was dreading the lunch. I had nearly changed my mind about attending due to finding eating in public an embarrassment and was almost on the verge of leaving now for the same reasons.

Since my treatment, I had been left with no sense of taste and very little production of saliva which caused my face to swell when eating; this made the process of swallowing food difficult and not at all enjoyable.

I had already given myself a good talking to on the way to the church and had come to the conclusion that I was amongst friends. Even so, it is sometimes difficult to be honest, even with friends and people you know and I didn't want to make a fuss and make people feel uncomfortable.

I was so relieved when I saw what we were having for lunch, because it was chilli and jacket spuds and I knew I could adapt it in order for me to eat some of it without unduly drawing attention to myself. Calorie counting went clean out of the window as I applied dollop after dollop of butter and crème freche to the mixture, and produced a lovely sloppy meal, fit for a baby, and one which would slip down my throat easily!

The acceptance and support of Cathy, (one of the Destiny team members), who was clearly sensitive to my feelings of unease, and the embarrassment I felt about sorting my meal, helped me to feel relaxed, accepted and loved. Therefore when my face swelled it wasn't too big a problem for me.

Feeling totally relaxed and comfortable, I sat and listened as the guest speaker started by singing a beautiful song and I found myself feeling that this woman's story was going to have an impact on me. What I didn't know was *how much* it would speak to me.

Her life story was a powerful and honest one and showed how God had brought her through a very difficult time in her life as a young woman. As I listened I was suddenly overwhelmed by a sense of responsibility.

I had recently been though a tremendously difficult time and had seen God work in a powerful and amazing way, but, did I have the right to keep it to myself?

At times throughout my treatment I had shared some of the wonderful things God had been doing with my church, but was it enough? Was this all what God wanted?

I'd often heard churchy declarations such as - 'it was just like a revelation', but in reality for me it was just simply as if a 'light had been switched on'. And it was now that I was seeing the power of my experience and how amazing God had been throughout my journey.

I left the women's lunch feeling excited about what God had done for me and with my mind flooded with words; I had an overwhelming desire to start writing down my experience.

Writing is not the easiest of tasks for me. I had been informed at the beginning of my attendance at university many years ago that I was dyslexic, but as I started to record my thoughts, I became aware that writing was not as difficult as I thought it would be, and although at times I found what I was writing emotionally exhausting, I was actually enjoying the experience.

It was only when my daughter Kelly read back to me an extract that I had written, that I realised this was not just a story of my journey through cancer, treatment and healing - but was much more than that. It was about a personal journey back to God. It was telling about how God brought me back into His loving arms through my experience, and had given me a deeper understanding of the true meaning of "being stripped of everything."

The Blue Settee

Stripped of my self reliance, my dignity, my privacy and my control, it tells of how I had no choice but to become totally dependent on Him as my Loving Father.

This journey has brought me into the awesome wonder of God's grace and forgiveness and has turned my life around completely. It has taken me through reconciliation, forgiveness and a much deeper understanding of His true faithfulness. It has given me a new sense of reality in my spirituality and a new sense of trust.

And I now have this urgency to share what I have been through.

The Blue Settee

As with most personal stories it's difficult to know where to start - there seems so much you want to say and so much to remember.

Prior to starting my treatment for cancer I had intended to keep a diary, but when the reality and the effects of my treatment hit my noble and positive plan, nothing materialised. The only thing that did materialise was a determination to survive and a hope that everything would be all right. Of course I had fear, but as far I was concerned, this new stage in my life could not possibly be as fearful or painful as what I had recently gone through in the last two years. Then, I had faced betrayal, deceit and a very painful divorce – something I had never thought I would survive – but I had and life had gone on.

Cancer had crept up on me slowly and silently.

For over a year I had suffered with the re-occurrence of a sore throat and excessive tiredness, which even had me thinking at one point that I had become overfriendly with various types of medication.

However, after three months of several mis-diagnosis by my GP, I became more concerned that something was seriously wrong. My persistence in seeking the truth resulted in me being sent to the hospital, where I was informed, unexpectedly, that I needed to return two days later with someone for support.

I was a little surprised by this.

The young man seeing to me had just asked me to open my mouth, but he wasn't really expecting to see anything, as he was only investigating a gastric problem. (My GP had thought that acid reflux was causing my sore throat, and they were looking at doing further explorations to confirm this.)

However, as the young man had looked into my mouth, he had clearly been able to see that there was a visible problem with my throat and neck. This confirmed my suspicions that something was seriously wrong and from that moment I had it in my head that I had cancer.

Two days later, Ron, my husband to be, and I sat in the very busy hospital room waiting to see the consultant.

This was where my first battle began.

First up was a junior doctor, who wheeled up to me on his chair, without so much as a how do you do, gelling up a foot long rubber tube as he did so! "Right Mrs Dixon," he announced, "I'm just going to pop this up your nose!"

Pop this up my nose? Was he crazy?

I recoiled in horror and up went my hand, right in his face and told him in no uncertain terms that one, I was not a "Mrs" anything, and two, there was no way on earth he was going to shove that rubber hose up my nose! I was here for someone to look at my throat, not shove things into my face!

The nurse and the doctor were shocked, Ron was mortified, but I was adamant. No matter how they cajoled and tried to persuade me, I was not going to allow them to do this to me. I was sitting there, with my nose pinched tightly between my thumb and forefinger, and my eyebrows brought together in a furious scowl – almost daring them to even try!

The young doctor beat a quick retreat gabbling that he was going have to speak to his consultant about this and my final words to him were, "You do that! Because that thing is *not* going up my nose!" and I sat back in my chair, my arms folded, much like a stubborn child.

After about five minutes of me sitting there sulking, the nurse returned to escort me and Ron into an office, where I was met with this massive desk and a huge consultant in a suit behind it, busy writing.

The atmosphere in the office was tense to say the least. There was a wall of silence from the consultant and he was surrounded by five trainee doctors who were all stood to attention like guards behind him. The consultant did not even glance up, even as we entered, and our escort, the nurse, quietly took her place behind us whilst we waited.

The Blue Settee

I was very much the errant child being ushered into the headmaster's office to await her punishment! Errant, and defiant, I have to say – ready to do combat with anyone who thought they could just perform any procedure they liked on me without so much as a "how do you do?"

It was a like a game of wills – me sitting there glowering hostilely and him sitting there totally refusing to even look up from his note pad, scribbling away in utter silence. I think he deliberately kept us waiting because I was clearly the "awkward patient" and needed disarming somewhat!

Eventually however, he decided to look up. As he slowly raised his eyes to look at me, his deep American voice was clearly disapproving as he said, "Mrs Dixon, I understand that you are refusing to let my colleague insert the camera to look into your throat."

"Firstly," I said, refusing to be intimidated by either the disapproval or the silence of his colleagues, "I am not Mrs Dixon. Secondly, I don't even know that man or even why he wants to put that thing up my nose. I have come here for you to look at my throat! He hasn't even told me his name or why he wants to do it. And nobody is putting anything up my nose! I don't even know who he is, or who you are and I am not doing anything until we've all been properly introduced!"

I nearly added "So there!" but managed to restrain myself!

At that point, he put his pen down, took a deep sigh and shook his head. He then turned to his colleagues and instructed them to introduce themselves. One by one they obediently delivered their name and professional title and finally the American made a big show of introducing himself too.

Five minutes later there I was, head back, tube up my nose and looking at a monitor at the inside of my throat!

Well all it takes is a bit of manners, doesn't it?

We were then told that we should return in a few weeks' time. They told us that they were ninety per cent sure that it was some form of cancer, but they would have more information for us in a few weeks' time.

This was what I began to see as our "naming" appointment and after a few more tests we found ourselves waiting once again to be seen by a consultant.

Eileen, the nurse who would become our constant companion throughout our visits, eventually appeared looking friendly and reassuring, and accompanied us both to the consultant's room.

I'm not sure what I was expecting when I entered the room, but I felt rather disappointed. Perhaps I had been expecting a large impressive room with a grand desk and an even more important and larger than life consultant - after all this was my 'naming' appointment.

Instead, what greeted us was a very young man, in a very small room, with a blue settee.

I remember being fascinated with the blue settee thinking it was a bit silly wedging this into such a small room. Before many minutes this young man was saying the words

The Blue Settee

'I'm sorry to have to tell you Mrs Dixon its bad news. The tumour in your throat is cancer.'

At that point all that came into my mind again was that he hadn't read my notes - because I was no longer a Mrs. Perhaps he had the wrong person or the wrong notes. I also found my mind wandering and thinking that the settee was very low. So, looking up at him was not very comfortable and actually was distinctly distracting because I was getting a worm's eye view of his very hairy nostrils.

Then I found myself rather bemusedly trying to work out whether he was telling me I was going to die.

After all, I knew I had cancer - I'd worked that out and they had practically told me as much at my last visit. So why was he sorry? It all felt kind of strange and very much like a dream. My feelings were real although a little subdued and I felt somewhat detached.

He announced the name of the cancer, but it had very little impact as I hadn't heard of it before. I think he must have asked if I had any questions.

As Ron proceeded to ask what, I guess, were the usual ones - treatment, survival rates etc, all I wanted to know was - what was next? What did I have to do to sort it out?

Perhaps it was my social work training, all that problem solving stuff that you have to do day to day.

I would like to say I thought of God but I didn't. All I clearly recall was my obsession with this blue settee and wondering how many people were given this type of news on it.

Much to my annoyance, the young man couldn't give me a firm plan yet, as all my notes had still to be sent to the cancer hospital at Sheffield. Here was where a treatment plan would be put together.

I felt frustrated and powerless by his inability to give me a concrete list of "to dos" that very day.

I found myself thinking "Why should I be expected to let *him* sort it out when he obviously was responsible for choosing this inappropriately sized settee for his room?"

Surely that was an indicator of how lacking in foresight he was? All he could give was "probably," "maybe," and "perhaps". Surely he had seen cancers like this before? Surely he should have more information than that for me? However, the only plan he was prepared to give me at that time, was to wait patiently…or maybe it should have been graciously!

Breaking the News

Even though I had known in my head that I had cancer, having it named somehow made it more real and the impact it was going to have on my family and friends began to become a reality.

Coming out of the hospital, we had a little time together where I reassured Ron that I was fine and I persuaded him to finish a work related call, promising him everything was going to be alright.

However, as I travelled home through the countryside, the truth of what had been said began to dawn on me and the fear of what the future held began to hit home. I stopped the car to give myself a moment to digest it all, as the tears began to fall.

Why me God? Why, after everything - the marriage breakdown, the divorce - why now? After all, my life had already been turned upside down once, and the emotional pain that I had endured then, had at last begun to disappear.

The belief and trust in certain people had slowly started to return a little; I had found a special man who I had fallen in love with (which was a surprise in itself considering I wasn't looking for anyone) and I felt like I had begun to live again.

After shouting at God angrily and telling him what I thought of him, telling him how disappointed and let down I felt, I then felt a sense of relief. I'm not sure why. Whether it was the physical shouting out or finding someone to blame, but nevertheless I felt better.

The tears began to dry and as I sat admiring the countryside, I began to recall my blessings. I had two wonderful daughters and two grandchildren and a new one on the way. I had found the love of a wonderful man with a beautiful and kind character, and was getting married in six months. I had some fabulous and supportive friends, however, quite how fabulous and wonderful people were I wasn't to realise until much later on in my journey.

As I have begun to write about my journey, four months after my treatment finished, I am reminded about how many times we're faced with difficult and fearful situations in our lives and often we can't see where God is – (which I have to say, I felt on a few occasions throughout my treatment!)

However, God had already revealed Himself several times up to the point of being given the results of my tests, and this had begun to restore my faith and belief in Him after the circumstances of the last few years had left me feeling very distant from Him. Although I had started to seek Him out by attending church again, I still felt pretty hard towards Him and, when asked about it, I had likened my feelings to looking through a window at all that was happening and not being able, wanting or even daring to open the window to reach out to Him.

When Ron and I were originally told by the hospital that they were sure I had a form of cancer, I decided there and then I would be honest with my family and friends. I had promised my daughters there would be no lies or secrets in our relationships, which was really important given the effects the divorce and the difficult issues we had had to face as a family.

I realised I had to be strong and I'd been told that half the battle was to keep positive. Sharing the truth of the possible diagnosis with my daughters was difficult and heart breaking. It's amazing how you can forget your children have become adults and how different and individual they are and how you instinctively want to try to protect them.

Kelly, my eldest daughter of twenty seven, lives in the Midlands with her husband Adrian and daughter Emmy, and had recently found she was pregnant with her second child, Abigail. Although Kelly, understandably, was upset and scared, she became quite motherly and protective towards me and her gentle nature had a comforting effect on me. Both Kelly and her husband Adrian attend church and I felt happy for them to enlist the prayers of their friends and believe in healing for me.

Paula, my youngest daughter at twenty five, and husband John and son Dominic, live in the next village to me. However, her reaction was totally differently. She was extremely upset and angry, and I found myself having to reassure her that everything was going to be alright. She took a little more time to get her head around it, but she became very positive and very much like me in terms of wanting to take care of the situation and gain some control. Her positive attitude was also very reassuring and, although I'm sure she was scared and had difficulty coming to terms with the news herself, she continued to be there for me.

As for my son-in-laws, they are as different in characters as my daughters are. They were wonderful and supportive in their own ways. Adrian, the very practical and God believing man, remained in constant contact with me and was very positive, and John throughout my illness, would text me to see how I was. He would just turn up to hug me and go away again; quietly showing me in his own way that he cared. I always felt that I was greatly blessed by having these young men in my family and, although both are very different, they remained very supportive of me, Ron and more importantly their wives. And therefore, I felt a great sense of peace that my daughters were taken care of.

The next hurdle for me was telling my sister Hannah. After sitting quietly in the lounge working out what and how to tell her, I telephoned her and after our usual catching up time, I took a deep breath and told her the whole story.

Initially I felt relieved that I had got through it and had been able to remain positive, however, by the end of the call I could hear that she was upset. Despite my best efforts to hold it together, I too crumbled and my positive attitude flowed from my eyes as my tears tumbled down my cheeks.

Looking back at this time, I think it gave me permission to cry for myself and acknowledge my fears and as sisters we shared a very special time together - supporting and loving each other. I was to find out a few weeks later why Hannah's tears were so heartfelt. I didn't know then, how God would use my desperate situation to work for the good of his children and undertake a wonderful and amazing miracle in my family.

As the manager for a Barnardo's Children's Service, the need to inform my Assistant Director of my situation early in my journey was important. Janette, despite her impressive title, has always been very supportive and has a caring and gentle way about her, which not only reflects the organisation's caring philosophy, founded in the Christian faith, but also makes the normal stresses of the responsibilities of my role more manageable.

I had worked with Janette for seven years and had developed a trusting relationship with her. This was reflected many times, but especially when I had had to inform her of the unexpected breakdown of my marriage two years before. Not only had that been the end of my marriage, but also the end of our thirty four year relationship. My ex-husband and I had been together since we were both fourteen. He had been with me all my life.

When telling Janette of the separation, I had tried to be strong and keep my information, as much as possible, to the point. I had wanted so much for her to see that I could cope because I needed to continue to work while going through my pain. Janette had been clearly upset for me and to see the tears in her eyes as she felt my hurt had been comforting and reassuring. She said that she was relieved as she had thought I had come to tell her that I was seriously ill.

However, I didn't know a few years later that's exactly what I would be telling her, and again I needed her support. Janette continued to be there for me throughout my journey and although you could say that I didn't need her permission to stop worrying about the Service or my job, and to focus on myself and getting better, it was extremely important to me to know that I didn't need to worry.

After telling Janette, I remember thinking 'Right that's another job done, what's next?" just as if I had been ticking off a list of jobs I had to do at work in a systematic way and then I began planning my next step. I did all this without really acknowledging or even thinking of the real seriousness of what I had been told, or maybe I just didn't want to face the truth and it was easier to deal with my situation in this way.

Some people were surprised that I was so open about what I had and that I didn't mind talking about it. Some were even a little shocked about how I came across so matter of fact, or when I appeared detached and emotionless at times, as if I was talking about someone else or telling a story. I'm not sure exactly why it was so important for me; to share what was happening to me; perhaps it was my way of coping and I suppose, looking back, that whilst I had been talking about it I had also been coming to terms with it.

Amazing Grace

My experience of hospitals had fortunately been very limited, having only given birth to two children, so the various tests and appointments I was requested to undertake were both bewildering and frightening. Having had an MRI and a CT scan, a full body scan was also requested.

I was extremely anxious when I arrived for this scan. I can't recall why this test was affecting me so much. Maybe it was the combination of having undertaken several tests, and with each one the realisation that of all the fears, my greatest worry and focus was the biopsy I was to have. Nevertheless my anxiety felt as though it was taking my breath away and by the time I had to lie on the scanner table I was close to tears.

I managed to control myself for most of the forty five minute scan and listened intensely to my new classical music CD. However, towards the end of the scan my anxiety began to grow. I started to feel desperately in need of the toilet, totally sick, and extremely fearful. My tears began to well up from what felt like every part of my body and my heart pounded in my chest. The more I tried to control myself, knowing that if I stopped the scan we would need to start all over again, the more I felt I was losing control.

The nurse working the machine became aware of my discomfort and tried to reassure me that I just needed to hang on for another five minutes. I remember feeling that she might as well have said forty five minutes as it didn't make any difference - I was desperate to get out.

I kept repeating to myself over and over again, "Why me, why me? I can't do this!"

When I had arrived for the test, a very quietly spoken young woman had led me into the room and then had just seemed to blend into the surroundings. I had totally forgotten about her. As my CD went onto the last song - the song which happened to be, of all the songs, 'Amazing Grace' - the strangest thing happened. I became aware that this song was now being sung to me by this young woman who was sitting at the right hand side of my head and her very gentle voice echoed the words to me in my ear.

Her voice was beautiful and calming and, as she sang, it was having a strange effect on me. I knew I was listening to it as if my life depended on it. I listened hard to every word, each one taking a new significance. The lyrics were no longer just flat, unmeaning but they felt as though they had come alive, and were so very real and comforting to me. An intense feeling of peace, warmth and wellbeing came with every sweet breath I took. Time, my desperation and fears melted away.

By the end of the song the scan had finished, and by the time I sat up on the table I only caught a glimpse of the young woman with the angelic gospel voice as she walked out of the door. I never had chance to thank her. And I never saw her again.

"Where Does My Help Come From?"

(Psalm 121 v 1)

After my initial tests, I remember sitting quietly in my office at work thinking and trying to come to terms with everything. So many things were going through my mind that I was jumping from one subject to another with no particular order to it.

How was I going to handle everything - the fear of the unknown, the treatment, and my faith? My silent conversations started to ask searching questions which had a slight sense of desperation to them, and from deep within me I felt I needed to find the answers.

I had become a Born Again Christian fifteen years ago and during this time I often heard people say 'It's ok for you but it's not for me' or 'People who are religious have God as a crutch.'

So if we use God as a crutch does that mean we are weak? Do we only want him when we are in trouble? When we are in trouble do we cry out to him and believe he is going to be there or is it just for comfort to *hope* he will be there?

I came to the realisation that I *had* to believe God would be there for me throughout this unknown journey, and if that meant God was to be my 'crutch' then I needed the 'crutch'. In addition to all the support and love I had from Ron, family and friends I knew in my heart that it was essential to my survival that I had something more, not only for me, but for my husband to be and my family.

I was asked if I would like to go to my church leaders, Mark and Carolyn's home to have a few people pray for me. I agreed. Although Ron was not a Christian he was more than happy for me to go. I must admit I was a little nervous. I'm not sure why, as I knew Mark and Carolyn really well and they had been there for me as others in Now Church had been, throughout my divorce.

To be honest I remember feeling a little uncomfortable in asking for God to help me when I had been so hard on him lately. This nervousness soon went when I arrived. I was so touched that Sarah, her husband Joseph and another young man called Justin were there.

I had known Sarah and Justin when they were young people in the Church and I had seen how God had worked in their lives. I was so very proud of them both. They had come to pray and believe for me, and knowing that prayers are a precious and wonderful gift costing nothing but love, I felt very touched. The prayers for healing, comfort, and for God to be there for me were very welcomed.

Although I was happy to try to believe for God's intervention, however superficially, my emotions were like a roller coaster. I still felt that I couldn't quite believe this was happening to me and was still hoping that I might wake up from the bad dream. None the less, I left the prayer meeting happy knowing that my friends were standing in for me, praying and believing for me - which was very encouraging.

When I look back at my plan of action it wasn't exactly a spirit filled, God focused, or even a faith believing plan, but I remember thinking that I had covered all areas of support for my little problem. I had got the support from Ron, my family and enlisted many friends - and had even covered the God angle. I realise looking back it wasn't really selfish and grasping at straws, but this was just survival.

And at least I hadn't left God out of the frame altogether!

But what I didn't know was that over the next six months God would reveal himself many times to me through my situation.

Chell and Shazza!

It wasn't just my Christian friends who rallied to support me. Indeed over the next few months I would really grow to appreciate the love and kindness of so many people in my world.

People I knew both at and through work were very caring and upset for me. Although at times I found myself being positive and comforting them, I felt this was okay and even a little helpful. You see, I was determined that I was not going to feel sorry for myself, and was going to take a proactive approach for as long as I could.

And determined to help me in my approach were two friends, Michelle and Sharron, who decided a Christmas shopping trip was in order for me!

That day I was dragged about all over as they treated me to a bit of retail therapy. But all I managed to purchase that day was two candle holders and three candles from the pound shop.

We had such a laugh but it was exhausting for me, and by the time we entered a dress store at the end of the day, I was dropping on my feet and my throat was swollen to ridiculous proportions, causing my voice to sound more gravely and husky than Rod Stewart's!

The shop was hot, sweaty and heaving with desperate housewives trying to bag a bargain and I had had enough!

In desperation, I began to croak out, "Make Way! Make Way! Woman with cancer!" Michelle and Sharron gasped at me in absolute horror and then just burst out laughing hysterically. Our antics earned us some bewildered and disapproving looks, but we did not care. It was an amazing release to laugh! It definitely is the best medicine!

Big Knickers!

The dreaded telephone call from the hospital arrived and the biopsy was booked.

Due to a last minute cancellation, my appointment had been rushed through and I had to arrange for Ron to meet me at the hospital later when he had sorted out his work. Maxine my ex sister-in-law offered to take me.

(She, together with her husband David, had always remained supportive and very much part of mine and my daughters' lives even after the divorce.)

While waiting for Maxine, I stood looking at my garden through the French windows.

November is not the prettiest of month for colours and interest, but I recall standing there for what seemed ages just staring and trying to remember everything, as if it was going to be the last thing I would ever see. The last few weeks had been an emotional time, all the tests and appointments day after day after day and finally, I had arrived for the final one.

My cancer at this point, I can honestly say, was not the biggest problem or concern in my mind. It wasn't even my main focus.

Fear of the future and the unknown was what troubled me the most. I had no idea how I would manage with the treatment, and this worried me. How would I cope? What would it be like? Would it hurt? Would it be horrible? What could I expect? I had nobody to ask these questions of, and even framing them in my own mind was sometimes too hard, too much.

But nevertheless I had experienced a lot of support from mine and Ron's family, as well as from my friends at church and work - and being able to talk things through with them, and being able to receive so much care and encouragement, really did seem to help.

I knew people were praying for me and I so wanted to be really positive and strong. And, although fearful, I tried to believe the prayers would help me to keep my fear controlled.

I had already met one of the surgeons and the anaesthetist who had both explained their roles, what to expect and possible side effects, but it hadn't seemed to make much difference. I hadn't asked as many questions as I felt I should have at the pre assessment visit because I had felt so numb, and by that time I was just going with the flow and wishing it was all over.

However, I arrived on the ward with Maxine, feeling fully prepared for battle. My fears were somewhat controlled and Maxine did her best to keep me chatting.

She was always good at that! She is definitely a woman's woman; very funny. And she chats about all the things that are of interest to us, and even when you don't feel like talking you're quite happy to listen. I remember feeling so grateful that she had this fabulous way about her, and having her around helped me keep my mask of positivity on. I even managed a laugh or two.

Before too long my well organised plan had tumbled into a heap. The biopsy had been brought forward. Maxine had already left and Ron, although near to the hospital, was held up.

I was going to have to face this all by myself.

As I waited alone to go to the theatre, the passing of time feeling like an eternity, my positive attitude began to waver. I tried to recall any scriptures, or words of encouragement people had said to me.

In my increasing state of panic I desperately tried to think if the ward name, "Elizabeth", had a special biblical significance for me, or if I had ever heard of a Saint Elizabeth, so that maybe I could feel I was being looked after by God and this was all in his plan. But to no avail, nothing sprang to mind. And as my fear continued to rise, I tried to do everything I could think of to prevent my tears from slowly flowing down my face.

I was curled up on the bed quietly weeping to myself, and at some point must have drifted off.

To my surprise I woke up still lying on my bed. It must have only been for a few minutes, but while trying to assess what was happening and whether anyone had noticed me, I found myself watching the woman in the opposite bed.

She wasn't doing anything particularly interesting just putting a few things in a plastic bag, but she smiled and said she was waiting for her husband and mother to collect her. Apparently she had been taken ill at the railway station while returning home to somewhere in Suffolk after visiting a foster placement in Chesterfield.

Enthusiastically I told her that I had also been a local authority social worker and was currently enjoying my job as a service manager for children who had been in local authority care. For a brief time I enjoyed my few moments forgetting my worries as we continued chatting and telling our stories. She went on to say that she had had to make do for two days while she had been on the ward - she had been forced to borrow a hospital night gown and she had no clean underwear.

I was more than happy to help her out as I had come prepared and proudly presented her with a new pair of extra large white pants - then I realised I was also embarrassed by the fact that these were not the size of underwear a woman of her age or tiny stature (or mine come to think of it), would necessarily wear. In my well prepared plan I had figured I needed underwear that was comfortable to lie in bed and avoid any embarrassing lumps or bumps.

When I explained this fact very apologetically and rather sheepishly, to my huge relief I found that she was still more than happy to take my gift. When I look back at this I have to smile. What on earth had I been thinking about? I had a problem with my throat, I was in hospital for only a minor operation, so why be so concerned with what I was wearing under my night clothes? And why did I decide to buy such large knickers, which in the end caused more bumps and lumps because I had to knot them in order to keep them up!

Nevertheless, after my room-mate returned to her bedside, the slight distraction she had provided me from my increasing fear was gone, and now it began to return and the feeling of rising panic started to have a smothering effect on my breathing. I vividly remember saying to myself "I can't do this, it's too much for me and why can't I feel that God is with me?"

I guess I must have looked scared because the woman returned to the side of my bed, and as I looked up at her, she placed her hand on me and said she would like to pray for me. It was a totally unexpected surprise, after all the only discussion we had had before this was work related, nothing to do with our faith.

After she prayed for me, she left me with her clothes in hand. I recall feeling totally shocked but my breathing and state of panic had subsided.

When she returned to the ward her family had arrived, and as they were all leaving her elderly mother walked slowly towards me smiling, and touched my hand and said in a broken English accent that she, her family and her friends at church would be praying for me. I was speechless, so overwhelmed by this act of love from a total stranger. Although my gratitude and tears came from my heart, as my words could not be heard, she smiled at me so reassuringly as though she knew what I was trying to say, and squeezed my hand.

As I watched them walk off down the ward, a nurse and porter arrived to take me to theatre. I then began the journey down the long corridors, but I remember knowing and feeling a sense of peace that everything would be alright.

The theatre staff were so friendly and before long I remember opening my eyes and listening to cheerful voices and laughter. And when I returned to the ward, to my relief, Ron was waiting for me. My tears were no longer from fear but from feeling totally loved not only by Ron but by God.

The Next Step...*Ron!*

The next day I sat at home feeling utterly relieved at getting through the biopsy with my right tonsil intact. I felt exhilarated and even slightly euphoric. I remember I was so pleased they had not taken my tonsil out as they thought they may have to do, which meant I didn't have to get over an operation before my treatment started.

I received what became normal text messages and telephone calls of concern, support and love. Although it was a little difficult to talk, I was more than happy to share my relief with my family and friends. It was around this time that I had a real sense of how important not only my family, which included Ron's family, were, but also how my friends would be so important to my journey and would have such an impact on me.

I guess what really touched me was the way Ron's family were so caring and rallied to support me – even though I had only known them for such a short while.

The Blue Settee

Many times throughout the next few months I was to be so touched and sometimes overwhelmed that there were so many people I had come into contact with through work, church and from the village, who would let me know how much they were thinking about me, encouraging me - offering support to Ron and myself both through cards and messages. We often take people for granted, but when you are faced with difficulties it's such a blessing to feel the love of people. This became tremendously important to me much later in my journey when the effects of my treatment began to take its toll and, at my lowest points, helped me to hang on.

After my blue settee day appointment there were two more things I had to do as part of my plan. The consultant had given me permission to visit my father and his wife, Carole, in Spain for a couple of days to tell him face to face that I had this illness. It was important for me to do this as he was seventy two years old.

I enlisted Kelly, Adrian and their home church, in addition to my friends from Now Church, to start praying for certain things. Flights to Spain were limited. Ron needed to have the time off from work to accompany me. The small surgical procedure being organised by the hospital needed to happen after I had been to Spain and finally, I needed my father or Carole to get in touch with me so we could tell them of our visit. This final point was very important as generally my father only contacted me once a month and he was not due to contact me. There was also no way of me being able to contact him.

As with all good organised plans I was prepared for change and flexibility, although strangely enough, I felt fairly confident that my friends' prayers would be answered and everything would work out - therefore I didn't worry.

So that left what I found to be the most difficult part of my plan to face, and one that caused me to lose a lot of sleep over.

As I sat alone in the dark one night, it felt as though the world had stood still and held its breath with the anxiety and uncertainty of my future. However, my uncertainty wasn't around the 'what if' question regarding my cancer, but about my future relationship with Ron. I didn't really have a choice about entering into this battle; but was it right for me to expect Ron to go through it with me?

To be honest I didn't have the right to expect anything from Ron, we were not married and we hadn't even been together for a great length of time; I could barely imagine what I would do if he couldn't fight this battle with me. As this thought caused all kinds of anxious feelings to well up within me, I continued to sit quietly and began to think of our history together.

It felt so important for me to examine, dissect and assess our relationship. Looking back and recalling my thoughts, I guess you could argue that perhaps I was trying to convince myself that my relationship with Ron was secure. I found myself trying not to compare him with my ex-husband's short comings, my experiences of being lied to and mistreated. I eventually realised this was not a positive road to go down as these memories and thoughts brought back feelings of my despair, loneliness and fear which were not helpful. After I allowed myself this short distraction I pulled myself together.

Ron was not my ex-husband, and nothing in our relationship gave me permission to compare them. I soon found myself smiling when I remembered that on St Valentine's Day I had sent him red roses with a card that said I would marry him. I had been so excited at the time; I had never done anything like that before or been so open with my feelings. Much to my embarrassment I felt I had acted like a 'giddy teenager'.

However, my eyes filled with tears when the reality of my situation struck me. I realised that it had only been nine months since that day, and all the excitement around planning our wedding and our future had disappeared into insignificance. As I desperately tried to get back on a positive train of thought, I looked back at when I had first met Ron.

I hadn't made it easy for him! My emotions had been all over the place due to the effects of the divorce, but he had become a fantastic and supportive friend.

I had told my friends and colleagues about him, and before too long, my non-existent love life and friendships were the topic of every telephone update and pre-meeting discussion! I was also receiving regular relationship counselling from my social services' agony aunts and my Barnardo's peers. I had often laughed and joked with my friends that the ideal man for me would need to be six foot tall and wear rigger boots, and be around my age. Don't ask me why, but that's what I had in mind.

But over time Ron's gentleness, kindness, sincere character and ability to make me laugh, brought something into my life that I realised had been missing for some time. But was Ron the man for me? He wasn't six foot - he was my very good friend. He was eight years older than me with grey hair and he definitely didn't wear rigger boots! How superficial and shallow we can become - especially when we wear a mask to hide our vulnerability and hurt.

However, the reality for me that night as I sat reflecting on my past and present was that I had to take the chance to face our possible lack of future together, and to possibly lose him. I know that people who knew Ron would have said that he wouldn't leave me to face this alone, but I needed to love him enough to let him have the choice, and although it wouldn't have been easy for either of us if he had to leave before the battle started, I felt I owed him this. As I cuddled up on the sofa with the next hurdle I had to face in my plan of action for survival, I eventually fell asleep.

While we were taking our usual evening stroll to de-stress from the day, there seemed to be an unspoken agreement between us that we didn't approach the subject of my cancer, so we embarked on polite and friendly conversations. However, the perfect opportunity to bring up our future together came quicker than I expected as we sat in the local pub with our usual pint and a coke after our walk.

Eventually the topic came around to my health. Our discussion started very tentatively as though we were being aware of what and how we were talking - each of us trying not to alarm the other by sharing our thoughts in too much depth. Up to this point we hadn't really had any 'deep and meaningful' discussions addressing our individual fears, our future or even the possibility of my death. We seemed to have just accepted the need for us to be swept along with the tide of circumstances, around the necessity for us to have a diagnosis, which had left very little space in our relationship to take time out to talk about "us" until that night.

While sitting and chatting I found myself being part of the conversation but drifting in and out of my own private thoughts, although listening to Ron and nodding and responding in the right places. My own silent conversation and thoughts were battling between bringing the discussion around to our future or possible lack of it, just leaving it alone, or facing it if I needed to at a later date. As part of this "inner fight" I also recalled Eileen our nurse saying to us both, when we received the news of my cancer that we needed to talk to each other and share our feelings and fears.

This silent battle was clearly causing me to feel and look anxious as Ron enquired if I was okay or just feeling tired? Before I realised, my mouth opened and a rush of words cascaded from me into a heap of emotions without me even taking a breath, or allowing a response from Ron before giving him, what appeared later to be, a list of reasons why he should not be around.

Ron, although visibly shocked about my outburst, simply took my hand and looked into my eyes and very calmly and gently said that he had waited eighteen years to find me and nothing was going to make him walk away. He was going to marry me but first he had to love me and care for me, and that he could do very well. My utter sense of relief was overwhelming and following my cuddle from Ron that made me feel so safe, secure and totally loved, he announced quite confidently a number of conditions he felt were important and that I needed to know.

With his usual cheeky smile he said that he could do most things but one, he didn't do 'sick'! Two, if I got mad at him, that was okay but could I practice saying sorry, as this was something I found hard to do. And for his grand finale, he asked if I would be paying him carer's rates and then giving him a reduction in rent when we were married? (It had always been a standing joke between us that I would charge him rent when he moved in with me!)

After putting Ron's slight misunderstanding of his future finances in order and his expected commitment, as instructed I practiced saying sorry in order to bank apologies up for later on. I reassured him he didn't need to do 'sick' and as we laughed and continued to enjoy each other's company, which included talking about our understanding of what was to happen, even making a few plans, the night soon passed.

I think both of us felt a sense of relief that evening, our laughter was so important to us both, a means to break off some of the chains of stress from our situation, as well as bringing something back to us that had always been very much part of our relationship. It was what made us strong as a couple - our ability to laugh with and at each other.

That night I fell asleep thanking God for bringing Ron into my life, and for how much this man loved me - enough to choose to enter into this unknown battle and journey with me. However, neither of us knew quite how important he would be in caring for me and what that would entail. It was perhaps a good thing, looking back, that God knew what he was doing bringing Ron into my life because nothing could have prepared us for what was to happen over the next few months.

Old Wounds

As expected, prayers were answered - our flights were booked and the telephone call from Spain arrived two days before we were due to leave.

I had been dreading the call, as I had no intention of giving the bad news over the phone. But when I told my father that Ron and I were coming over for a few days and needed to talk to them both, as I had been a little under the weather, he took the decision out of my hand by asking me outright if our visit had anything to do with my throat.

His question put me on the spot, especially when he explained that he and his wife, Carole, had recently watched a television programme on throat cancer and had compared my symptoms with the ones described on there.

Apart from telling him an outright lie, I felt I had no choice but to break the news to him and, in a way, it was a relief that the task had been made easier not only by his phone call, but by his direct questioning.

Even though I tried to reassure him that everything was going to be fine, and that I would be bringing with me all the information for him to read, it was still difficult for me to leave them to come to terms with this news – knowing how much he would worry.

Cancer, I have realised, is such a dreaded word in our culture, and for my father one that caused him a massive amount of fear.

Prior to me leaving for Spain, I sat having a drink with my sister Hannah, and while sharing my thoughts about my cancer I had a sense of relief and took comfort in the fact that that we were now in regular contact with each other, and having a sister in my life again was great.

I feel at this point I need to explain how my family "looked" to the outside world.

You see, my parents divorced almost forty years ago and I have three sisters, but over the years the bitter effects of the divorce, resulted in what has become the 'norm' in our society as a "parental and sibling" split. This meant for us - 'natural' family relationships could occasionally be difficult, and over time the split had unfortunately become an accepted part our family life. The dividing line between us seemed so strong and clear to me, that family events, such as marriages or christenings, often caused me stress and emotional hurt. It appeared to me that my sister Hannah and I were on one side and my mother and younger siblings were on the other.

Eventually the day had come when I had been faced with the prospect of both my daughters marrying, and inevitably my thoughts had turned to the future where, at some point, precious little ones would come along, and I had had to ask myself - was it right that this accepted family split, which had caused me hurt and sadness in the past, be passed down into another generation?

I had felt it was time to make a difficult decision. The pressures and split within my family had become too much for me to cope with, and this meant that I had had no choice but to walk away from my mother, stepfather and three sisters.

Looking back at that decision I can't say it was the right or wrong one to take, only that, at that time, I had felt this was the only path I could follow to get me off the emotional rollercoaster that was attached to my family life. But what I can say was, it was a decision, though not easy, I had had to learn to live with.

Several months prior to my illness starting, I had become aware that my family were going through a difficult time due to my younger sister, Avril's, tragic loss of her forty-three year old husband, which had left her with two small children without a father.

However, as Hannah and I were chatting, I felt as though she somehow had an insight into how I was feeling and after our usual family chats talking through each of our children's lives – and also moving on to talking about my sisters Avril and Penny and their children, she said that she had something she needed to share with me.

She then went on to tell me that Steve, my mother's husband – our stepfather – was battling cancer.

As I listened to the terrible news, all the shortcomings I felt that my family had, including my own hurt, became insignificant and for a few moments I stepped into my mother's shoes. How would I have coped when all that was important to me as a woman and a mother, was thrown into a spiral of fear, uncertainty and pain - painting a tragic picture?

How would I have coped with all of this?

In the space of two years, she had supported a daughter who had lost her husband to a deadly illness, she had been dealing with her own husband's losing battle with cancer – and now, she would have to face the news that her eldest daughter was starting her own journey with the disease. It was so unfair and although my mother was a proud and strong woman, I felt devastated for her.

As I sat in disbelief I listened to how Hannah and husband Peter had been helping to support my mother, stepfather and sisters through this time, and how the family had pulled together. I agreed to Hannah finding the right time to tell my family of my battle, thus avoiding the possibility of them hearing from another source, and my agreement to perhaps the possibility of meeting them again.

On my flight to Spain, lost in my thoughts, I looked through the window at the bright nothingness scene and I felt confident that Hannah would talk my family through my situation in a loving and prayerful way. However, what I didn't know was that God had his own picture to paint and he was to use this desperate and tragic picture of a family, to paint a new one of hope, reconciliation, forgiveness and love.

Spain

As I saw my father and Carole waiting for us through the glass door at the airport, my feelings were a mixture of relief and anxiety at seeing my father. Relief as sometimes we secretly feel our 'dads' can sort anything out, and anxiety, because I knew that every detail would be demanded of me from my father. I knew that he would want to analyse and dissect every bit of information I had been given, and to go over every letter, of every word, of every conversation. My father would want to know everything!

I realised this was a perfectly natural thing to go through but at the same time I knew as well as supplying details of my illness, I had to be positive and reassuring due to my father's age.

Truth was though; no amount of trying to whitewash this would make the reality go away. I was facing the biggest trial of my life, and the unknown journey stretched out ahead of me and there was no other way but to move forward into it.

While travelling to the apartment our conversations were a little stifled due to everyone trying to maintain composure. My father and Carole were obviously trying hard to hold it together, and as for me I tried to appear a picture of health and both Ron and I were trying to be very cheerful.

However, when we placed our bags in the bedroom and sat down to a drink, this signalled the start of the long road of information sharing, reassuring each other, facing our fears and planning. I found the next couple of days extremely emotional and physically draining and with each discussion I hoped that my father could see that I was going to be alright.

I'm not sure who I was trying to fool by my positive attitude as it was very clear that I was struggling with my health. My medication had been increased for the pain in my throat, resulting in me falling asleep a lot, which was a new addition to the extreme fatigue that overwhelmed me continuously, something that had everyone alarmed – not least of all, me.

When I got up through the night to top up my pain relief, at times I would find my father sitting in quietness or on other occasions he would find me sitting in the dark and thinking about things. This gave him chance to spend time coming to terms with what was happening, although I found myself getting irritated because all he wanted to do was keep talking and analysing everything, which I found slightly negative. I so wanted to be positive but, secretly I was trying to hang on to the slim silver thread of belief that God was in this battle with me, to help me keep my fear from utterly consuming me.

It was a huge relief one afternoon to get away from facing my cancer for a while.

I sat overlooking the beautiful scenery from a village high up in the hills, quietly lost in my own thoughts. Everywhere looked so perfect and beautiful, but within all this beauty I found myself again asking, "God, why me?"

I'd never been a smoker or a big drinker, I hadn't done anything bad to anyone; I was a good person and a good mother.

I became aware that I watching a small bird sitting on a bush near me. For a few moments I felt so envious of its carefree life and its expectation that all its needs were being provided for. Surely I could remember something in the bible after all my years as a Christian that I could take comfort in and say this scene had a spiritual meaning for me! Was there something about a bird in scripture, something about worry or was it something about clothes?

But after a few minutes I smiled and thought to myself, "I've failed again to muster up something deep and meaningful from the bible!"

It made me chuckle to think that I couldn't have been listening during the many hours of sermons and bible readings at church through the years, if I couldn't even recall if there was something in the bible about a bird. As I laughed to myself, I confidently gave myself a logical reason as to why this was the case. I must have been worrying about my Sunday dinner burning during the sermons, so obviously I just hadn't been paying attention!

Strolling down the small narrow roads with their pretty cottages we were obviously all enjoying the time out and even managed to have a few laughs. I remember thoroughly enjoying the snapshot of people's lives as I looked into the windows of the cottages. However, at the end of the road I caught a glimpse of my face in the window and for some reason I recalled a scripture 'Trust the Lord with all Your Heart'.

I knew there was more to it, but this was all that was important to me.

I had first been given the scripture when, as a young Christian, I had decided that it had been the right time for me to be baptised.

Unfortunately, there had been an issue that had prevented me from moving on. You see, I had learnt to live with the sexual abuse I had suffered at the hands of a family friend but I hadn't been able to move away from asking God why it happened to me, why was I still being plagued with emotional outbursts and flashbacks.

However, the week before my baptism I had listened to a visiting speaker who had talked about her own experience of childhood abuse, and like me she had been asking God "Why?"

I remember the overall message really spoke to me. And by the end of it, I knew I needed to trust God and not to keep asking him "Why?"

I realised there were some questions that I would never get answers for and so I needed to put it on my "Why?" shelf and stop wasting precious thoughts, emotions and time in trying to find reasons.

But one thing I could be assured of was that God would always be there for me. So, I had got baptised and had believed that I would be healed of the effects of my abuse.

I can honestly say my problems associated with my abuse were never really a problem after that day, but this had been tested a year later when I had spent the afternoon at the Charter day in my local town. In the hustle and bustle of the crowd I had become aware that I was standing next to the man that abused me.

I'm not sure if he had recognised me as I looked into his eyes, but I knew it was him. I just stood frozen in time as I watched him slowly walk around me. As my eyes followed him as he left the street I become aware that I had no feelings of anger or fear, just a calmness that had given me a reassurance and comfort that the chains that had bound me from my abuse had truly been broken. It had been the first time that I had experienced the amazing power of God's healing.

Remembering this miracle gave me determination never again to ask God why I had cancer and, from that day on, I just took each day as it came and lived it as it was given to me, however I felt, or whatever happened.

On the fourth day of my visit to Spain, my assigned nurse, Eileen, was due to call to relay to me the results of a meeting the consultants had to discuss my treatment. I was expecting my treatment to take six months which would take me past my proposed wedding date, something I was desperate to avoid.

The beginning of the week arrived and throughout the day we had kept ourselves busy avoiding discussions around the possible information I would be receiving from Eileen.

As arranged, the call came through. I listened and tried to absorb every bit of information that was being relayed to me and as I stood cocooned in the moment of the urgency of my illness, standing in a busy Spanish holiday resort, trying to come to terms with what was a major event in my life, miles from everything that was 'normal,' it felt very surreal.

Eileen confirmed to me that the tumour, which was attached to my right tonsil, had spread to the back of and under my tongue and into three of the lymph nodes in my neck. She informed me that the tumour was too big to operate on and any surgery would be far too invasive; therefore the treatment plan was set for an intensive three month plan of radiotherapy and chemotherapy.

After the call ended I wasn't sure whether I should be happy, relieved or worried that they couldn't operate, so when Eileen telephoned half an hour later with an appointment date to see the consultant on my return home, I informed her of my mixed feelings.   She spoke positively about the treatment plan and said I should be happy, as the plan was a curative plan and would not be palliative at this point. She then went on to say that in layman's terms, which was echoed by my consultant at a meeting when I returned home, that 'they had one chance and one chance only to sort the problem out, therefore they were throwing everything at it!'

Although this gave me an immediate sense of relief for a short time, as I relayed this positive plan to Ron, my father and Carole, I began to absorb the seriousness of 'one chance and one chance only'. For the first time I saw that my death could become a reality.

As we walked around the shops, I remained numbed by the enormity of the information, going through the motions of sightseeing, continuing to wear my mask of positivity, yet at the same time secretly trying to make sense of everything and come to terms with my possible death.

While trying to see through my tear filled eyes, staring at non-descript items for sale, Carole had become aware of my failing positive stance and, as we huddled in a corner away from everyone to regain my composure in order not to upset my father and Ron and draw attention to myself, I pulled myself together. I walked out of the shop repeating to myself again the only scripture I could recall *'trust the Lord with all your heart'*. To be honest, at this point, I can't say trusting the Lord with all my heart was easy to believe or do, but at the time it was the only thing I had! By saying it whether I believed it or not, I hoped it would make a difference.

Despite the intensity of the five days away in Spain, Ron and I did manage to find a little time to relax, forget and enjoy a bit of sunshine and later, as we sat at home looking back at those few days, we were both relieved that the plan now included extra support from my father and Carole who were returning early from their six months in Spain in the new year.

The four of us had spent quite a few hours trying to work out a plan for the next few months. My father, had wanted to come back with us immediately to begin taking charge of my care, but Ron and I had persuaded him that until my treatment was actually underway, we would be fine.

We agreed that he was to help drive and accompany me to the hospital each day for my treatment, and he also took charge of an exercise plan he believed I needed to have which he felt would help me fight my way back to health. Carole would keep the house going and Ron would look after me at night and at weekends. This sounded like a good plan of action, because I knew my father needed to feel in control to some extent, and this would help him cope as well as support. I was pleased that the last pieces of jigsaw had been slotted into place for the next few months so now all I needed to do was to concentrate on the next round of tests, hospital visits and my family contact.

Coming Home

My return home also brought back the reality of not only my battle with cancer but with my step-father, Steve's battle with the disease. I had already made up my mind that one of the first things I should do in the New Year was to be there for my mother and sisters.

After telling my father of Steve's illness he felt very strongly that I should contact my family and began to lecture me on the importance of getting in touch with them. My father's always been good at bossing me about and I've always been a good daddy's girl. He made me promise to do so and it was not a difficult promise to keep. After all, this was something I needed to do for myself as well as them.

I'm not sure what I was expecting or why I felt a little apprehensive about my visit to see my mother. I had already tried to imagine how it would go, what would be said etc, but the visit went really well and on the way home I sat recalling the events of the visit.

I had always seen Steve as the gentle giant, but what I found was just a shadow of the man I knew. Still a gentle man but one who was fighting his battle with dignity, and as for my mother, she was still a proud and strong woman, but she also had a softness to her and it was clear that she was also clinging onto her husband's life. Steve had remained positive about my diagnosis while we were chatting and this helped me face my fears.

Sitting there with Steve I had the strange sensation of looking in a mirror and seeing me in the months to come. It was not a negative experience because he was positive and serene. He always believed that I was going to get better. This positive spirit and the contact we began that day remained during my treatment. Something special happened that day which took all the bitterness of the past and caused it to simply melt away. We were now on a journey as a family which would take us down a road that would heighten our need to be together, supporting and loving each other through the next few months.

As expected, my hospital appointment took me through my treatment plan. However, the consultant's statement 'one chance and one chance only' didn't have the dramatic effect as it did before. Because I had heard it before I felt much less panicked and somehow I felt I was more than prepared.

The telephone call arrived from Eileen saying that my gastric 'peg' could be fitted on Christmas Eve. I was happy to have this done before Christmas as I did not want the prospect of this procedure hanging over me during the Christmas season, and I was aware it was not going to be a very pleasant experience. Having a small tube inserted into my stomach was a vital part of my preparation. I had been told that when the treatment took hold it was very likely that I would not be able to eat or drink, and that most of my medication would have to be applied intravenously via this tube. In effect the gastric peg would become my lifeline. And because of this little friend of mine, I would eventually become affectionately known at work as "Peggy Sue."

I agreed to attend the ward and with the usual prayer support I arrived feeling confident although a little apprehensive, and without really knowing or understanding what the procedure entailed, I listened carefully as the consultant started to talk me through it all.

As he spoke, his words began to hit a wall of disbelief, horror and fear! Somehow, throughout the many times I had been made aware that I would need to have this procedure done, I never thought to ask what or how - or maybe they told me and I had not been really listening.

"You are not doing THAT to me!" I told him in an outrage and flung myself out of bed wagging my finger in his face furiously. I was blustering and red faced and just could not believe that one human would dream of doing that to another – even in the name of medical science!

If the consultant was shocked or appalled at my behaviour he didn't show it and he continued to remain calm and professional, and although I did not appreciate it at the time, I look back now and see that he handled the situation sympathetically and caringly.

Shortly afterward Eileen arrived on the ward to see me. She was met with a flood of tears and after she hugged and cared for me, she again talked me through everything. I agreed to it but only if she would be with me, which she was more than happy to do.

When I arrived at the theatre, as promised Eileen was waiting for me. The scene that was set reminded me of the many times I watched hospital programmes - with lots of professionals gathered around a patient in a disorganised organised way, each with their own role. I can't say it was a particularly pleasant experience; however the sedative enabled me to relax and listen to Eileen's words of encouragement and to detach myself a little from what was happening.

Christmas Eve, at seven o'clock, I was allowed to leave the hospital.

As I waddled down the corridor, holding on to my stomach like a pregnant woman protecting her "bump", Ron holding my arm so tightly he was practically carrying me on one side, we arrived in the reception and were greeted by a family with two small children running around wildly. Ever protective of the protruding peg – I scowled warily at the youngsters, fearful that they would barge into me and dislodge my new attachment.

Ron left me propped up against the wall outside whilst he went off to fetch the car. He returned moments later to find me sprawled out on a bench. Thrown into instant panic, he yelled at me to "stay where you are!" and launched himself back into the hospital searching for help. Typical Christmas Eve scenario – nobody around, so poor Ron was flying up and down looking for help.

Finally he found a security guard and between them and the casualty staff I was soon being bundled into a wheel chair and whizzed back inside.

The panic we had created caused the two young children, who had watched Ron and I shuffle by a few moments earlier, to now gape at us in wide eyed amazement. What they thought of our dilemma was soon to be revealed.

"Mummy, mummy!" One cried as we scurried past, "is that lady going to have her baby now? Like baby Jesus?"

It was later that the funny side would hit me. Right then I was feeling distinctly bad tempered and out of sorts. Apparently I was suffering the side effects of the anaesthetic but until they took blood from me they would not know for sure, and I was determined nobody was sticking any more needles in me that day. Nobody!

I was like a stroppy teenager sitting there, peg sticking out of my belly, bottom lip protruding even further, crying and making a fuss and declaring myself at war with anyone who came near me with anything remotely resembling a needle. Ron was beside himself as he encountered Susan in her 'Little Miss Independent' mode for the first time!

Eventually Ron pleaded "I want to have Christmas dinner at home!" and threatening, "You'll have to go back on the ward!" He finally managed to win me over, and reluctantly begrudgingly I gave in.

When the nurse tentatively poked her head round the door to see how his "persuasion" tactics had gone, Ron proudly announced, with a massive smile of triumph on his face, "I did it! She'll let you take the blood!"

Christmas morning Ron and I were faced with the task that became a daily ritual of looking after my 'peg'. Ron had taken on the role of 'chief cook and bottle washer' and went to prepare for task. As for me, I lay on the sofa waiting gingerly, not knowing whether it would hurt when we had to 'flush' this thing out.

I'm not known for my bravery. I was the only person in my daughter Paula's beauty class that couldn't go through the leg waxing as it was too painful, so the prospect of this was not good at all. As I tried to talk myself round knowing that this was really only the start of things, Ron appeared at the lounge door.

How do I describe what I saw? Immediately my fear was totally swept away under a wave of hysterical laughter as my eyes fell on Ron, who was standing there with what he later described as in his scrubs - hairy legs, black socks and 'Shreddies', white shirt worn backwards and makeshift mask, tea towel draped over one arm and holding aloft a large syringe full of water in the other hand. That was so typical of Ron doing everything he could to allay my fears and it worked! I laughed so much, it took us both some time to recover.

Needless to say I forgot my fear and we followed our instructions methodically.

As we talked over our first Christmas dinner together I realised that God knew me so well. If I had known how traumatic having the 'peg' implanted into my stomach was going to be, it would have spoilt any chance of 'normality' over Christmas. Although I had to be careful not to catch my stomach as it was quite tender, at least I didn't have to face the fear and dread throughout the Christmas week. You wouldn't have expected anyone to have had a nice Christmas and New Year with such a dark cloud hanging over them, but this was not the case for me. I had a lovely time and was shown so much love from family and friends throughout the week, including a lovely New Year's eve, that as I faced the New Year count-down I recall feeling it counting down to my year of hope.

A little Miracle

I had agreed to be part of a research programme so all my tests had to be done twice.

The Consultant's Registrar informed me that they had decided not to give me a session of chemotherapy prior to my treatment starting, to ensure I was as healthy as possible for what he described as a gruelling few months ahead.

As the registrar checked the previous scan results, which had initially shown the three infected lymph nodes in the right side of my neck, he seemed to take some time flicking between the two results. After a while, he felt my neck and again re-checked the latest results.

Finally he turned to me and explained what he was now looking at and showed me how the first set of results had clearly shown the cancer to be in three lymph nodes. But the second set showed that the cancer was now only in one.

Strangely, I wasn't sure at first what he was saying, so I asked him if this was good. He assured me this was very positive. It wasn't that I was disbelieving him or that I didn't believe in healing, I just hadn't expected to hear or see this, and to be truthful I hadn't even contemplated healing through the many prayers that were being said for me!

Anyway, I just smiled at him and calmly, almost jokingly stated that I must have been healed. He smiled back at me and said, "You never know!"

As I walked out of the room, the reality and excitement of what I had seen and heard utterly amazed me, and with hope overflowing from me, I couldn't wait to tell my family and friends! Suddenly as I walked into the bright sunshine – I felt a huge WOW! And an overwhelming sense of hope and amazement! It felt like a new dawn, a new day!

New Year 2009 – The İron Mask

Right at the beginning, from my diagnosis, I had a determination in my heart to maintain as much independence as possible. This meant that I would try to attend hospital appointments under my own steam. It was something that I felt I needed to do.

When my first marriage ended, I could not even set my own alarm clock such had been the level of dependency on my ex-husband. I had only realised how dependant on him I had become when the marriage was over. This scared me. I was left at that time feeling totally out of my depth and out of control.

In the months following his departure from my life, I built myself up to such a high level of independence I was determined never to give that up, or to grant control of my life over to any other person!

It became more important to me as the months went on, and I would politely refuse offers of help to accompany me, stating it was not fair asking people to sit about waiting for me when I was happy to go it alone. In truth it was important for me to feel a measure of independence and control.

In January I arrived at another hospital appointment on my own. I was due to have a mask made for me which would fit around my head and neck. The radiotherapy would focus and be directed on the locations written on the Perspex mask.

I had been made aware that this could be quite claustrophobic so, as I lay on the table while the nurses made a plaster cast impression of my head and neck in order to make the mask, I was determined not to panic. It was not particularly pleasant. I had to concentrate hard while the work was going on, especially when my face began to be covered leaving only a little space for breathing.

When you are fearful you can become so aware of how your body is reacting. I recall that although I only felt a little anxious, I could hear my heart pounding in my chest, I could feel my heavy breathing and I was acutely conscious of my clammy hands.

In fact, as I lay there waiting for it to set, not daring to move or breathe very much, my hands were gripping the blue paper towels on the bed. When it was all over the paper towels had become screwed up tissues in my hands and were stuck in blue patches on my palms.

As I kept my eyes tightly shut, I started to recall the things that had happened to me over the last few months that confirmed that God had been with me through some scary moments. Just as though I was watching previews of movies, I encountered each amazing incident one by one, and again the scripture that was to stay with me throughout my journey – *"Trust in the Lord with all Your Heart"* - enabled me to hang on, lie still and keep calm.

The day arrived for my final appointment with my consultant and pre-treatment visit to the radiotherapy suite for my 'practice run'.

I had agreed to my father accompanying me and to allow him to ask my consultant questions he felt he needed answering. At this point I felt it would be helpful, but later into my treatment this was to change.

Parking in the hospital car park and walking towards the large austere grey building, I felt very small and insignificant. It reminded me of my first day at school - everything looked big, important and scary. I had visited the hospital many times for appointments but that day it all felt very different. Actually on previous occasions the building had not been grey in colour. Today however the building seemed to absorb all the grey bleakness of the day, sapping all of its sunshine. It seemed to symbolise all of my most despondent thoughts and fears.

The "iron mask" (although made of Perspex) was proudly presented to me. My nickname for it came from the movie of the same name and was equally as unpleasant to wear as the one in the film had been. When it was placed on my head it clicked together with a loud crack that startled me. I never did get used to that sound, as it signalled that I could no longer move, and although I only had to let the radiotherapists know I needed to get out, it still made me feel anxious when placed on and around my head and neck. Even thinking about it now causes me to cringe. It felt like a death mask!

As I lay on the bed very still in order for the radiotherapists to undertake their final check for measurements, my feelings were a mixture of anxiety but also amazement at the technology around me. Everything was so big but at the same time graceful. The movements of the machines were so smooth, like the arms of the most elegant dancers folding over me, to undertake the most precise delicate operations. It was fascinating and distracted me from the actual treatment. These enormous machines took the measurements that would ensure the laser treatment only affected the parts of my throat, tongue and neck that needed it. It was scary as well as intriguing how precise those measurements were.

The final step I had to take before starting my treatment was to meet the consultant who I would be meeting with weekly during my treatment.

This man turned out to be the very larger that life professional I was originally expecting to see at my blue settee appointment. Even my father was impressed!

He was everything I imagined he would be. Tall, dark, immaculately presented in a "Saville Row" style suit, with shiny Italian leather shoes, and an equally larger than life watch to suit his personality! He was instantly recognisable as someone to look up to, not only by me but by his staff. It was very clear from them that he was held in such high regard, they said he could "almost walk on water!"

When he spoke there was such an air of authority that it left me in no doubt that he knew exactly what he was talking about. And yet there was an extreme gentleness in his mannerism towards me as his patient, that caused me to have faith that if he was telling me everything was okay, then I could be assured that it was. But likewise, if there was something concerning, I knew that it was serious. I would, however, only find this out later.

In his hands I felt so safe.

My father asked his questions and was happy with the answers he received. I didn't mind him asking and to be honest it gave me another chance to absorb some of the information I had missed at other meetings.

Light at the end of the Tunnel

The night before my treatment was to start I lay in bed unable to sleep. Half of me was relieved the day had almost arrived; the other was dread, uncertainty and fear of the unknown journey. As I looked into the darkness and caught a glimpse of the street light through my curtains, I smiled as I thought of the well known saying "there's a light at the end of the tunnel."

In my silent thoughts I asked whether I *really* knew if I had a light at the end of my tunnel. I knew that God had shown himself to be with me in some amazing ways over the last few months, and I felt so blessed to have family and so many friends supporting me and praying for me. So, was it right to place a lot of confidence in my consultant? Did I have as much confidence in God now the reality of my treatment was to start? I wasn't sure what I expected God to do; was I expecting him to heal me of the cancer? Did I have enough faith when tough times were to come to hang onto him? Was I a strong enough person to hang onto life, and what was expected of me? I had been told many times how strong and positive I had been over the last few months, but now the reality of the treatment was to start, would I be able to hang onto my belief in God?

My mind was flooded with questions and thoughts but what about answers? What about comforting and positive thoughts to help me and lead me into this unknown battle?

While staring into the darkness my thoughts drifted into a story that had really touched me many years ago, a story which I had never forgotten. I had first heard it at a youth conference I had attended with the young people in our church. It was about a battalion of soldiers who recognised God as their saviour.

The emperor, who had no faith in God, wanted complete allegiance to him and so wanted all Christians to renounce their faith in God, even the Christians within his own army. Some of these refused to do so.

The order went out that all soldiers refusing to renounce their faith in God were to be stripped naked and forced into the centre of an iced covered lake. This done, the emperor had his generals in the army surround the lake with hot steaming baths - to tempt them with the promise of life and warmth if anyone would renounce their God.

The general of one particular battalion of Christian soldiers pleaded with his men for hours to renounce God and be saved. He valued his men so much and just wanted to save their lives. He could not understand why they would just not renounce their faith in God.

As one by one the soldiers slipped into the melted lake, their life snuffed out like a flickering candle, the general's infuriation at the "stupidity" of his men turned to deep respect and sorrow. He knew that their faith was so strong, they would never renounce their God, and though he did not fully understand, he could only admire their faithfulness to their God.

However, as the hours passed and more men disappeared into the icy black lake, the fear, the cold, and the desperation seemed to just overwhelm one particular soldier, overcome with fear, he ran off the lake into a hot bath, renouncing his faith.

The general, having been so taken aback by his men's love of their God, saw this and felt such pity for the man, that he took off his own clothes and armour and took the fearful soldier's place in the middle of the frozen lake - and there he stood with his men as they entered the gates of Heaven, joining them in an act of bravery for the poor soul who had not been able to stand the test himself.

Remembering this story, the answer to my question was already firmly placed in my heart. If I could not stand firm in my belief and faith in God over the next few months, during my battle for life, my family and friends that had been with me through some dark times, would take my place and stand firm and believe that God would be there for me. An overwhelming sense of peace enabled me to close my tear soaked eyes and rest in God's love until morning.

Morning arrived and in a quiet organised way, the final preparation took place for my journey to the cancer hospital for my first chemotherapy and radiotherapy sessions. I had to take an overnight bag due to being part of the research programme which meant that with each chemotherapy session a stay in hospital was required.

As I travelled through the early morning rush hour in silence, I remembered the contents of a card that had been sent to me by a young social worker I had worked with for a few years who had experienced her own fight for life. Two statements she had written in her card had blessed me and throughout my journey I would often allow the words to soak into a moment in my experience. She had said that it was okay to cry but to cry with dignity and that colours that can be seen everywhere would never be so bright. Both statements were so very true, that morning even though it was overcast, the colours and the wonders of the nature I caught sight of were so rich and had a depth of beauty I had not really seen before.

The Battle Begins

Arriving at the ward I felt like the new kid at school, with their mum and dad in tow. Everyone appeared to know the staff and what was expected of them and by contrast I didn't even know whether I needed to get changed, sit on the bed or the chair. I felt so awkward and obvious, as if everyone was looking at me and waiting for me to make a mistake and even perhaps break a rule. Eventually the nurse took me through the expected routine of this visit and, hanging onto every word, I tried to absorb the information so that I too could fit into and blend in with the routine of the ward.

Preparation for my chemotherapy, which was to take place through the night, went ahead and my attendance for my first radiotherapy session was not particularly eventful. Although as I sat waiting for my name to be called in the reception area, I closely examined every other person sitting in the room, wondering what their cancers were? Were they ill? How were they coping?

Everyone seemed relaxed and a few appeared to have made acquaintances and as I nosied in on conversations, I tried to work out if there was anyone here with the same problems I had.

As my name was called, I followed the nurse to start what became my routine procedure. However, I was relieved when my first radiotherapy session was over. I hadn't expected it to hurt; I had been told that it would be about two weeks before I would start to feel any effects of the treatment, but I left the radiotherapy suite quite proud that I had done it and had held my fear under control and myself together. One down thirty four to go.

As I returned to the ward, I didn't feel so conspicuous and after my father and Carole left, I lay on my bed listening and watching the other women on the ward. The afternoon went fairly quickly and was uneventful. I had seen a couple of friendly faces; one of the research nurses had come to see me and I had spoken to my consultant. I had received the first round of text messages of support and even managed to have a snooze.

After Ron left me in the evening, my chemotherapy treatment started with the usual bags of saline and then in the early hours of the morning the chemo, followed by more saline. When breakfast arrived I felt great and started to eat the cooked breakfast I had ordered. Everyone else seemed to be enjoying their food but before too long the side effects of the chemotherapy began to kick in.

I started to feel ill and the breakfast that I had just been enjoying didn't stay with me for long as nausea and vomiting took control. This took me by surprise as I hadn't expected it. After all I had taken the anti-sickness medication and up until that point I had been feeling fine.

After several attempts by the staff to stop my sickness with different treatments, I eventually found relief from the effects and was eventually allowed leave to return home with my instructions and follow up medication. Although I had not had the most pleasant experience, due to my body's reaction to the chemotherapy, I again left the ward feeling fairly proud of myself that I had coped so well.

On the way home chatting with my father and Carole - we had lots to talk about as we all felt that this was the first hurdle we had jumped - I suddenly began to feel very unwell.

My father and Carole had been almost military like in their planning and preparation to cover any eventuality. Ron and I had laughed when we first saw how much thought they had put into to it. The huge bag they had put together and squeezed into my tiny Mini Cooper had an assortment of items to take care of any unexpected events. There were bottles of water, baby wipes, sick bags, towels, tissues, clean underwear and even, to my greatest embarrassment, a small baby changing mat to sit on in case I had an accident. Oh yes, and of course several black bin liners.

The Blue Settee

All the preparation had seemed excessive at the time, but it had kept my father occupied and feeling useful so I didn't mind too much.

And it turned out, as I found out on my first returning trip from hospital; the reality was that we did need to be prepared. And that big lumping bag turned out to be my life line throughout my treatment, as my body was to react badly to the treatment plan.

As the next few days went on and the effect of the chemotherapy settled down a little more, the daily routine of travelling to the hospital for the next two weeks came and went with few problems. I had my customary sleep in the morning after I returned from the hospital and then embarked on my exercise plan that my father had prepared for me.

Initially the exercise plan seemed to be a good idea, and I was very enthusiastic about it. I could certainly see the logic behind my father's thinking.

However, the effects of the research drugs, combined with the radiotherapy and the chemotherapy were such that my body was unable to retain food or liquid. A few weeks into my treatment, I found that the constant draining of my body, the sleepless nights staggering back and forwards to the bathroom and the general feeling of being utterly unwell weakened me, so physically, even the thought of carrying out the exercises was too much for me. I had lost so much weight, so quickly and was still losing. All I felt like doing was sleeping.

They gave me extra medication; trial medications, and new medications all in an attempt to control the sickness, but to no avail. No matter what they gave me, it just came back. Their constant nagging at me to keep eating was awful – how could I eat when my throat, already terribly sore from the radiotherapy burning away the tumour, was being irritated further by the effects of vomiting so frequently? How could I face food when I knew that it was barely touching my stomach before presenting itself to me again? Why wouldn't they listen to me when I was saying to them the fluids I was putting into my body were being expelled almost as quickly as I was putting them in? All anyone could seem to say to me was, "eat more, and drink more!" I felt like screaming, "Somebody please listen to me!"

Emotionally and physically I was beginning to feel absolutely wrecked. My daily routine had changed so that we saw Ron giving me my mixture of medications at five thirty in the morning through my 'peg', and this included him melting the research drugs to a thick liquid consistency in order for me to be able to take them. It was these research drugs that became the bain of my life.

Not only was the medication making me physically sick, but even worse was looking at the repulsive fluorescent sludge. It was disgusting and made me literally retch at the sight of it – especially first thing in the morning. I began to dread Ron coming in with them and would get really stressed about it – and in order to avert tears and stubborn refusal to cooperate, Ron would enter the bedroom hiding the drink behind his back so that I could not see it. He was like a patient father trying to medicate an errant, fearful and often uncooperative child!

And for heaven's sake, I wanted to scream – had my throat been able to withstand it – what on earth was that disgusting smell emanating from me?

I had begun to notice the smell just after the first month of radiotherapy treatment, but what had started as a strange whiff, was now becoming really offensive to me! It was also becoming apparent to others. Nobody had told me this would happen! I was mortified to think that poor Ron had to endure this – I mean, what man wants to be with a woman with permanently bad breath? Every time I opened my mouth the whole room would be filled with the scent of decay! I was horrified that I was causing the smell!

The consultant explained what had happened. The radiotherapy works in the same way a microwave works on cooking a chicken. The chicken flesh will yellow and curl, and this was what was happening to the flesh in my mouth. Unfortunately, as the flesh had begun burning away, an infection had set in, and this was what was causing the horrific smell. Literally it was the smell of rotting flesh!

This just added another woe to my growing list of discomfort and misery. I was getting weaker by the day, my mouth, tongue and throat were excruciatingly sore, I was excessively tired, had very little ability to talk and now this! What else could go wrong?

Father and Child

In my desperation to have a break from the constant diarrhoea, Ron and I decided that I would stop taking the research drug for the weekend, which I had been told I could do. This gave me some relief and I felt that I had regained some control of the situation.

My father, however, was not pleased with my decision and, being already deeply disappointed that I had been unable to continue with his exercise regime, I felt a strain beginning to develop between myself, my father and Carole. Things were coming to a boil between us, especially as he was aware I was considering not continuing with the chemotherapy, which he felt was a sign I was giving up. And although I realised that he was frightened for me I felt I needed to be guided by my consultant.

Having my father and Carole living with us and being so actively involved in my care plan had seemed like a great idea, and having them live with me six months of the year before Ron and I got together, had caused me to believe that there would be no problem. Ron and my father had always got along so well. However, that was before I became ill.

I felt that my illness and treatment had become secondary and their need to take control of me and my situation had become their priority. I had ceased being my father's grown up daughter and had become his little girl again. I understood this, as he just wanted to take care of me, but as my journey progressed it felt like it was becoming far too intrusive. Every appointment with the consultant and dietician he and Carole would attend with me, and although this was fine at first, the private conversations I had with the consultant, and the discussions we had, my father seemed to feel he had the right to challenge. And any advice they gave me, he took on board to mean that he should ensure I followed that advice. His methods however fluctuated, between feeling like bullying and gentle encouragement, which I found hard to cope with emotionally and I desperately wanted him to understand how it made me feel.

I understood that his fears and frustrations were making him appear even more bullish than usual, but his outbursts were becoming more frequent and more difficult for me to cope with. He took any decision I made as a direct snub and a sign of ingratitude for all of the things he and Carole were trying to do for me, which then caused his over-wrought emotions to overspill, which created a very difficult atmosphere.

Looking back I realise that, at times perhaps, my behaviour had probably reverted back to a child-like stubbornness, and I needed to be 'strongly' encouraged by my father. I think that Ron's gentle nature helped to balance out my father's fighting spirit in the beginning, but the more poorly I got, the more frightened I think my father became, and the balance tilted.

I realised even when my health was at its lowest point how much they were doing for me, and despite all the tensions and outbursts, I knew that this was an extraordinary situation and one which no one should have to experience. Certainly no one can be fully prepared for, or can even imagine how they will cope in such extreme times. Therefore in reality, until you come face to face with this type of survival and pressure, you don't know how you will cope and the best you can do is simply do your best. My father was doing his best. He felt he needed to use his spirit and determination to fight for me. However, what he didn't understand, and perhaps I didn't fully appreciate until now, was that God had got me in the palm of his hand and was allowing me to take refuge in him.

The tension between the four of us was exacerbated by the lack of space and privacy and my weakening physical state brought it to a head. Some days I barely had the energy to crawl out of bed, and certainly the state of my mouth and throat made talking a nightmare of an ordeal. Consequently I lost all motivation for anything other than sleep. I would drag myself out to the car, for my daily treatment at the hospital, but for the most part, all I wanted to do was hide under my comfort blanket and sleep.

Ron tried his best to act as mediator between the three of us by reminding them that it was my right to stop the research drug, and that it was my right to consider which options were best for me regarding my treatment – even if that meant considering stopping the chemo. At the same time Ron kept reminding me that my father was just frightened. However, an unfair comment and observation made to Ron by Carole brought it all to a head.

Ron by nature is a gentle man who would prefer to avoid confrontation and to keep the peace, but the comment was enough to push him to call us together in attempt to resolve the mounting tension. My father however seemed to be in no mood to try and resolve anything.

Barely giving us chance to explain where we were coming from, and rebuffing Ron's attempt to clarify that he was not trying to tell my father what to do, he launched into an angry tirade of accusations – telling me that I had given up, and that taking myself off the research drug, considering stopping the chemotherapy, and even the way I looked – were all indicators that I was giving up the fight, and he was disappointed in me. He felt that I had lost my dignity; that I was slobbing around in clothes too big for me; when I walked I walked with my head down; and that nobody else in the hospital waiting rooms looked as bad as me. Everybody else was coping with it, why couldn't I?

He couldn't seem to see that my clothes were hanging off me because of the weight loss I was suffering, that my head was down because the treatment, the constant sickness and diarrhoea and the lack of food and fluids in my system, were just taking its toll.

My father had "fought back from a stroke," and wanted me to display the same fighting spirit he had shown in doing that. I could understand where he was coming from. The problem was, even though I couldn't physically show I was fighting, inside I was only just managing to fight my way through each day, and at times barely believing in life itself.

I knew that my father was scared and thought I was giving up, but eventually I made him see that what was needed was not for me to pretend to be OK, but to try and make the consultant see that I was unwell, that I was actually getting more and more poorly by the day. And that I needed help.

This consensus that we finally reached after an emotive few hours, did seem to take some of the tension out of the air, and probably gave my father a new focus. Come hell or high water he was going to make sure somebody listened to him!

I lay in bed that night feeling so relieved. But I was also very hurt. Why could my own father not see how poorly I had become and how I was struggling with each day. On the other hand, there was Ron who had a quiet caring way about him, who didn't need words to see inside my thoughts and see my struggles and fears. I really believed that God had sent Ron to me for such a time as this!

Wigs

When it came to my appointment, although my father stood by me in the consultant's room, it was actually me who managed to make him see just how poorly I had become. When he looked at my weight and he saw how much it had plummeted and listened to my symptoms he realised that something was very wrong. Immediately I was booked into the ward where it was discovered I was severely de-hydrated. After weeks of trying to tell them all that I knew something was wrong, I felt such a huge sense of relief that finally they were taking notice of me. I had been heard.

Sitting on my hospital bed trying unsuccessfully to be brave, I was somewhat embarrassed by my tears as the nurse desperately tried to find a vein which was, as usual, hiding. The scene looked like something from the children's ward with mum and dad in tow trying to comfort and encourage their child to be brave. After what seemed like an eternity

The Blue Settee

I was finally attached to my lifeline and after bidding fare-well to my father and Carole and contacting Ron I lay back on my bed.

Here I was again, the new one on the ward. Feeling relieved to be here, yet emotionally drained, I scanned the other five women. I'm not sure what for, other than I felt thankful that everyone looked well and normal and obvi-ously visiting time was soon to arrive. I don't remember falling asleep but it must have been for a while because as I began to come round from my rest, lying with my eyes closed, listening to the women's conversations on the ward, I became aware that visitors had been and gone.

As I slowly opened my eyes and began to focus on my surroundings my heart leapt with shock and disbelief at the unexpected sight that faced me. I sat up in bed and tried to focus on what had happened. My disorientation must have been apparent to the women as they tried to reassure me but all I could manage was a polite smile. How could this have happened to me? Why would they have moved me onto a ward with sick people while I was a sleep?

My surroundings looked familiar but I didn't recognise anyone. These women had no hair and were all attached to life lines, and they looked so ill!

When I scanned the ward again each woman began to look a little more familiar. The penny began to drop. The woman in the next bed was gently brushing something in her hand. When I focused a little harder I realised that she was brushing her wig and, in fact when I looked around the room, I saw that each woman had a wig sitting on their bedside cabinets like magnificent and majestic trophies.

I gently lay back on my pillows; my tears flowing. In my desperation to hold myself together, preventing my emotions from bursting out, I reverted back to a childhood trick, closing my eyes and hoping that I was invisible to all around me, and praying that my fear and bewilderment was just a bad dream.

You see, up to this point I had managed most of the time to avoid accepting the reality of what was happening to me. I had got used to referring to my illness as nothing more than being a bit poorly, but coming face to face with the reality, and having to cope with my feelings of bewilderment and disbelief when looking at these women, was hugely difficult.

Even then I tried to disassociate myself from what was happening. I can even remember thinking to myself that they had only put me on this ward because it had a spare bed. Also I hoped that I didn't make the other women feel uncomfortable because I was not and didn't look as ill as they did. How wrong was I?

When I looked in a mirror I did not see what others saw. All I saw was that I was a bit red in the face from the radiotherapy. I never saw how baggy my clothes were on me, or how thin I had become, or how much hair I had lost. I thought I looked OK. I actually thought I looked really well. I certainly would not have placed myself in the same category of illness as these women. Perhaps I should have been more honest with myself, or perhaps I just did not want to see; perhaps it was a fear thing. That by seeing it I would have face unpalatable possibilities.

It was only near to the end of my treatment when talking to my Macmillan nurse that I truly realised how ill I was, and that realisation was so devastating for me that I felt that my body became one tear, a single cry of anguish and fear. I could not believe I had been so sick and so near to death.

Lying on my bed on the ward with my eyes tightly closed, I became aware of laughter and excitement in the tone of the voices of my room-mates. I then heard the words, "Spirit, God and Son" and as I sat up I realised that they were talking about attending their own churches. One woman even talked about her son having an experience with the Holy Spirit. The woman in the opposite bed looked over at me and asked which church I attended.

I found myself sitting up in bed with an almost silly smile pasted on my face, and 'I can't believe this' muttering under my breath. Listening to how excited and how positive they were about God's healing and looking at how these brave and sick women, whose bodies were being ravaged by treatment, still believing in healing, and were able to be laughing and talking positively about life. How could this be?

They had so much life in them and were so full of hope, and this seemed to overflow from each one of them and infect everyone else. It was contagious.

I soon relaxed and joined in the discussions telling them about my amazing experience with the nurse singing in my ear and shortly after my feeling of devastation, bewilderment and fear once again melting away. I was now experiencing the feelings of hope, comfort and safeness.

Oldest Hippy in Town

Arriving home feeling positive after my experience on the ward and a little better in my health, I soon got back into the usual drudge of the day - being woken up at five thirty am, being force fed the gloopy fluorescent gunge, and trying to drink something. I would get up and get dressed at seven fifty five and not a moment before. You see, between my early morning call and eight was the time to get myself mentally prepared for the day. Often I so wanted to give up, stay in bed, sleep and not have to face the day, the treatment or the routine.

With military precision my routine would have to be followed. Eight o'clock was my deadline for leaving the bungalow for my daily radiotherapy treatment, travelling up to an hour in the traffic to Sheffield. My father would have the car running to warm it up, so all I had to do was drag myself to it carrying my box of tissues, my comfort blanket and my sick bowl, and then I would curl up on the back seat of my Mini Cooper.

Once I had been delivered to the treatment area all I had to do was wait patiently to hear my name being called. When my name was shouted, my response was to whisper my address and date of birth. Every other week this routine slightly changed. The nurse would play the normal game of hide and seek with my veins for the blood tests; I would then catch up with the dietician, and finally see the consultant.

Only weeks into my daily routine, the effects of the treatment started to have what had become the usual effect on my body, and each daily visit to the hospital began to get harder, and my morning preparation time became almost unbearable. On my return home, sometimes all I managed to do was flop into my bed and snuggle into my comfort blanket for the biggest part of the day.

My father and Carole would ensure I got up in the afternoon so that I could lay in the lounge over-looking the garden and, between them, kept my medication and cleaning of my 'peg' up to date, until Ron arrived home to take over.

Magnetised to my fridge door was my chart depicting my daily countdown to the end of my treatment, and before long it showed that my next chemotherapy session was due. My consultant had already spoken to me several times about his concerns around the side effects on my body from the treatment plan, and although he seriously considered stopping the treatment, he decided, after we had talked about it together, that he would try and reduce the strength in the hope that it would have fewer side effects afterwards.

So the day arrived for my second chemotherapy and as I marked the date off my list with my marker pen, I felt confident that I was going to cope better. I had been to church the day before and thanked people for all their prayers. I had needed to take extra morphine because I was so determined to let people know that their prayers were holding me up, and to tell them how much it helped to know that people were behind me, even though I struggled to pray myself. I was so touched that they cared enough for me to do it on my behalf.

My second bout of chemotherapy was as bad again as the first one. The sickness and diarrhoea had become uncontrollable again. Eventually they gave me extra injections to help my sickness and diarrhoea, so after a few days they allowed me home which was great as this was also my forty-eighth birthday.

I sat at home on the settee, feeling pleased with myself, although I was feeling very weak from the sickness and lack of maintaining very little fluid in my body, the great thing was, I had made it home, and I had got through another chemotherapy session.

Although, Ron had always been good at fussing around me, that day he had become even more so - continually ensuring I was comfortable, taking care to brush my increasingly thin and lifeless hair and suggesting clean socks (even when they were already clean!) Part of me wanted to enjoy the fussing, but another part, the 'Little Miss Independent' part, was slightly annoyed - after all, I could still change my own socks, comb my own hair and if I felt like it, I could even make the decision to leave it all alone!

While sitting with my little grumpy and slightly ungrateful head on, I heard a knock on the door and could hear a bit of a commotion in the hall. When I looked up Ron was standing with a smile plastered to his face and from behind him there appeared a sea of large black fuzzy wigs. I couldn't believe my eyes! Here were some of my friends walking into the lounge, all dressed up, singing happy birthday with plates of food, a bottle of wine and pressies!

I was so overwhelmed by the love and affection from them all. I lay on the settee, not able to talk too much and not able to even eat. I sat and watched and listened to everyone really enjoying each other's company and it was great for a short time to forget how I felt.

Barry, my senior practitioner from work, looked the funniest. At sixty four years old you could have forgiven him for acting in a more gentile way and in a manner more befitting his age. But that's what made it more humorous to me. He appeared to relish the whole dressing up thing and threw himself into his character totally - he was certainly the oldest hippy in town! His wife Yvonne, a very beautiful, gentle and kind lady, kept him under control and occasionally reminded him of his age.

My shopping mates Michelle and Sharon, with hubbies Nick and Andy in tow were as always full of life, fun and laughter - things were never dull with them around. Paula, who I had gotten to know a little more personally at work, also popped into see me with her husband Simon. She had been a tower of strength during my initial assessment period. She had been able to empathise fully with my inner most fears, having had experienced a similar journey of her own. This meant for me that while I had been working, she had been able to recognise when I was struggling and was able to offer support. This, with the extra support from Barry and my other senior practitioner Stuart, had meant that I had been able to keep my head above water at work until I left to start my treatment.

Ron also appeared to enjoy all the laughter and fun, and the stress and heaviness in his face lifted for a short while, and his visible relief was very evident to me with every laugh.

When the party initially started, I caught a glimpse of my father's face through the lounge door window. He was obviously not happy with my visitors arriving. However, shortly afterwards he and Carole were helping Ron act as host. It was only after everyone had left that I realised his main concern was that I was not well enough for visitors. He was also put out that he had not been informed of the "surprise party" and would not have agreed to it, had he been asked.

Ron had not thought to say anything to my father when they had telephoned to confirm they would be over in a short while. This had not been done maliciously. You see Ron had lived on his own for eighteen years and was not used to 'getting permission' or seeking views from anyone before making decisions and genuinely didn't think about it. He'd simply thought it was a good way of cheering me up.

Although not consulting with my father was perhaps only an oversight on Ron's part, it just seemed to bring another stress into our situation. I realise that everyone, including my father and Carole, were all just trying in their own ways to make a difference. However, the fragile threads that were holding our relationship together were continuing to fray.

I really enjoyed my little party and, after an hour or so, everyone left and although I was extremely tired, it had been so nice for Ron and me to just have a little break from my illness. Even though it was only a short break from the emotional stress we were experiencing, it was needed and very much welcomed.

Pants and Needles

Before too long I was taken back into hospital again because I was still having difficulty in retaining fluids. This visit saw the focus of my wedding in May become an important part of me coping with the effects of the treatment, the daily struggle to survive, and would give me a little silver lining of normality around my dark cloud.

My first stay in hospital was the only time where I was put on a ward with other women. After that, I was given my own room. Although this gave me a little more privacy, there were times when I felt isolated and alone, and it was a little scary sometimes, as I would lay watching and listening to people visiting the room next to me who were unfortunately losing their battle.

I spent many hours in this room over the course of my treatment, just staring out of the window, listening to the business of the ward or sleeping, and at times it was very hard to be positive and see life after my treatment. Feeling so unwell and struggling for survival soon becomes a way of life, and the more simple things of life, the things I had always took for granted before my illness, things like hope, positivity, or the ability to laugh became harder to find. But as usual Ron would come up with a little gem knowingly or even unknowingly at times that would cause me to chuckle, and bring a sense of normality back into my world.

As usual my veins were playing hide and seek with the nurses. I had become increasingly fearful and upset with this game, and even the thought of it would cause a tearful reaction from me. I would lie on my bed for several hours, sometimes praying that they would either decide I would not need a cannula putting into me, or that a vein would miraculously decide to co-operate for the first time. Neither option seemed very likely.

The dreaded statement from the nurse "let's try and find a vein that wants to play today" would kick-start the normal chain of events – me holding back the tears, feeling sick, and I would even strike up inane conversations, rambling on in the hope that it would buy me more time, delaying the inevitable for as long as possible. Sometimes I would get myself so worked up I would even start to feel faint.

As usual you could see me reverting back to my childhood, forgetting that I was now a grown adult, and not even the nurses' powers of persuasion when they stated "Come on Susan, this isn't going to hurt!" were going to work, because I knew fine well, it would hurt. And I was right. It did hurt me!

To my relief Ron was with me this time. After all he was a caring man, and was always encouraging me and tended to my every need. As the nurse started the usual routine of trying to find a vein, keep me calm and focussed on other things, so she tried to bring Ron into the conversation. Ron had a tactic designed to refocus me. He would encourage me to think about our wedding, our reception and all the preparations.

In keeping with this the nurse was asking Ron about our wedding, where it was, our honeymoon etc. In my desperation to try to possibly buy myself time I answered all the questions quickly, which left Ron with nothing to say. I remember looking at Ron and whispering sorry, and said to him to carry on and to please help me get through this. Just the sound of his voice was always really helpful and I needed distracting from what the nurse was doing.

However, Ron appeared to be busy shuffling around a very small space between the bed and the wall. I wasn't sure what he was trying to do, but trying to keep an eye on the nurse and where the needle was in relation to my arm and also trying to fathom out what Ron was up to became very difficult. The needle won and while watching it slowly make its way towards my arm, I shouted to Ron "You're supposed to be encouraging me and helping take my mind off this!"

To which he replied in a muffled voice "Oh, err, yeah, um, just think about the "Breeze Inn" having a pint overlooking the sea in Tenerife".

As I looked to see where he was, all I could see was a man in a peculiar position, bent over my hospital bag rummaging around, trying to find something, although I'm not sure what. He continued his encouraging conversation, offering other suggestions but obviously talking into my hospital bag on the floor. When I enquired what he was doing he informed me that he didn't like needles and it made him feel sick at the sight of them.

I didn't know whether to be mad or laugh at this sight, but when he stood up, his face flushed with colour from bending over and standing proudly before me, presenting my spare pair of very large 'prepared for any emergency' knickers in hand, which happened to have been left in my bag from my biopsy visit. Both the nurse and I burst out laughing. I wasn't sure what was the funniest thing - Ron's embarrassment at holding up the large knickers, or the fact that he didn't like needles. Needless to say I forgot the problem I had normally with the nurse locating a vein and I found myself attached to my lifeline.

Unexpected Storm

Returning home once again, feeling a little stronger and again having a sense of; "I can do it, I can keep going," - my life very quickly went back to its normal routine. Over the last few months I had received so many cards, texts and telephone messages of encouragement and there had been so many visitors - from work-colleagues, friends from church and my family (which now included my sisters, mother and stepfather) all of which helped my life remain bearable.

My health once again deteriorated and the pressures on Ron were visibly taking its toll. I later discovered that he had confided in his friend stating that he wasn't sure if he was going to a wedding or a funeral. My father and Carole had given up trying to get me to eat as it was obvious this was no longer possible, and it became more about how much fluid I was able to get into my body and how much I could retain.

The Blue Settee

My medication now included stronger morphine, which meant that it had to be administered regularly as well as my other medication due to the amount of pain I was having. The thick florescent sludge had been reduced in the hope that some of my symptoms would subside. The smell of decaying flesh that was part of my life became more apparent and I had become more embarrassed and upset about it. Day and night seemed to roll into one due to the amount of time I was sleeping, which became very disorientating.

Ron would come in from work to take over from my father and Carole. His first job was to sort out my medication, and then he would have his tea and a shower. His routine would see him almost carry me to the bathroom and help me have a bath. It was so important to me to continue to do this as I felt I still needed this little bit of normality. Although, I have to say that at times I got frustrated when Ron would be too gentle, treating me as if I was made of glass in case he hurt me, which was lovely of him, but it didn't get me dry! Ron soon discovered the art of interpreting "the look!" He would dress me and then carry me to my bedroom, and then he would sit quietly at the side of me on the bed.

I had become so weak due to the constant loss of fluid and found talking nearly impossible. I didn't have the energy to do anything, just sleep, but when I woke up I would open my eyes and he would be sitting next to me quietly, holding my hand. All I could do was smile at him and fall asleep again.

Despite having to get up every day for work at five o'clock, every four hours through the night Ron would give me morphine, in between other pain relief. If I was sick or had another accident, he would just quietly sort things out, not making a fuss to embarrass me more than I already was, and he would do everything to comfort me when I cried. At these dark moments he would gently remind me of our wedding plans and encourage me to focus on the future and how wonderful it was all going to be. No matter how hard it was he never complained, he just quietly went about his business, caring for me, doing what he promised me he could do.

One day, after my usual radiotherapy session, the vomiting began again, but this time would not stop! No matter what we tried, I was just continuously throwing up. This went on all day and by eleven o'clock at night I was totally worn out.

While Ron was helping me, my father took control and contacted the hospital. After some discussion about whether I should be admitted that night or wait until morning, I decided that as I was due in any way I would wait until then. To my relief they recommended that we get a GP on call to visit that night and give me an injection to stop the sickness. This was not as easy as we first thought it would be. Every telephone number we had been given over the last couple of months had no response, and the answer from the NHS Direct Service was not helpful, giving us advice which had us going round in circles ringing different people and getting nowhere.

It soon became apparent that my father was increasingly becoming frustrated and angry while on the telephone trying to sort things out. The desperation in his voice echoed the feelings of us all, however after an hour of unsuccessful conversations my father's frustration exploded.

As I lay in my bed waiting for Ron to return with some water, my father stood at the bottom of my bed, looking so frightened, lost, and helpless. His desperate plight to get help for his daughter then spilled into his conversation with me, and before too long I lay listening to him telling me he thought my sickness was in my head and I needed to calm down.

When I challenged this as best I could due to my difficulty in talking and vomiting, he was in such a desperate state of mind, that although he was standing in front of me, he could not hear my words, and in his agitated state even suggested that I was "causing trouble!" and quickly rebuffed my attempts to calm him down.

This was a difficult and frightening time for us all and the growing sense of increased desperation, and the sense of totally losing control of everything, was immense. Each of us was slotted into a role - Ron quietly focused on looking after me and, at times, totally ignoring the scene that was playing around him; Carole was trying to calm my father down, trying to keep the peace and maintain an eye on Ron and I, and hoping that neither of us would react to my father, as she did not want us to make things worse.

My father was trying so hard to sort it out, but it was obvious that he was not coping with the frustration or the situation. I on the other hand was too ill to shout, but after a while all I could say to myself over and over again was, "trust, trust, trust!" I had nothing else left but to believe I was in God's hands. I was frightened and desperate, but as time went on and the situation was still not resolved, I just lay holding Ron's hand and hanging on desperately to my Hope.

We can all react like my father, even if we believe God is in control of our lives, and especially when we get frightened, faced with the unexpected and especially when it involves someone we love and nothing we do can change the situation we are in.

Through the years I had read and listened to many stories from the bible presented in church, but one that I have recalled many times talks of Jesus and his disciples in a boat on a calm lake. Unexpectedly a storm blows up and very soon the boat was surrounded by large waves. The disciples had seen the miracles that Jesus preformed, but still they experienced fear and as the storm grew, in desperation, the disciples woke Jesus up from his sleep. He listened to his disciples' pleas and despite their lack of faith, he calmed the sea.

God had shown me that He had been with me during my journey in some amazing ways but with this new storm I experienced a new fearfulness and felt a more intense sense of desperation. But, I have to ask myself now, what if

I hadn't had my faith, even though at the time it had felt as small as a mustard seed and that hanging on to it had been incredibly hard?

My father, unlike me, had absolutely no trust or faith, and his feelings of uncontrolled desperation, fears and frustration was hard for me to witness. I had to trust, I had nothing else - and clinging onto faith, as my deterioration in health brought me to my lowest point – what would I have done without trusting God? Looking back I realise now that even a mustard seed can grow.

To the relief of us all, the doctor arrived a couple of hours later and thankfully the injection calmed things down until morning.

The journey to the hospital for my radiotherapy session was a silent one. Relationships were fragile. I was upset to think that my father thought that this sickness was all in my head, and although deep down in my heart I knew he was just frightened, I wanted him to trust, but I knew he wouldn't.

After my session, my father and Carole helped me to my room where the nurse was waiting for me, and left to go home. The fear that was usually present and all the problems associated with finding a vein wasn't part of this admittance to the ward - I felt too weak to care.

Hooked up to the drip administering fluids to my system once again, I lay on my bed having barely the energy to open and close my eyes, and drifting in and out of sleep. I could overhear muted discussions from concerned professionals who were stood around my bed, talking about the increasing deterioration of my health.

I was experiencing a feeling and sense of illness I had not felt before. I became aware of my breathing, my heart beating quietly and the lack of strength to be even bothered to turn and look at the people in the room tugging and pulling at me.

Alone again, staring out of the window in my room at a grey sky, it appeared to reflect my sense of calm and my feelings of the nothingness of my existence. I started to think of my life, my children, my family, and the man I loved and was to marry in three months' time. I wasn't fearful or desperate - I just felt warmth within me and an acceptance that this was my time to leave the ones I loved. I no longer had the strength to fight or to carry on.

As I closed my eyes again to sleep, my mobile phone which was tucked under my pillow made a noise. I slowly brought it to me and as I looked at the small screen a message from my friend Liz, said: "Susan, remember what God has said to you: Believe in Him, trust in Him, find your strength in Him, take refuge in Him and remember his promise to you!"

As I smiled weakly, I knew that this was not the time for me to leave Ron, my children or family and friends, and as I fell asleep once again I knew that God was with me.

The nurses looked after me through the night and kept me comfortable and clean. In the morning the consultant, his registrar and students came to see me. He informed me that they had had a meeting and that he felt that I could no longer have chemotherapy. He spoke in professional terminology to others in the room and then sat on the bed and explained that unfortunately my body had had enough and was now no longer coping with all medication, all treatments, even the liquid food.

I remembered that we had had a similar discussion a month ago, but this time something he said made me think it was different. I can't really remember exactly how he explained it, but I remember hearing the word mortality, and I knew by the look on his face that he was concerned.

I had managed most of the time to avoid the acceptance or contemplation of death, but now lying in the hospital bed, half of me was listening and the other half did not want to hear him explaining everything. Was I looking at death?

After he finished talking this was the signal for me to thank him politely and watch them all leave my room.

I lay quietly hardly daring to move, his voice and his words whirling around my mind. Did I really understand what he was saying? The nurse, who had been in the room with the consultant returned, sat on my bed and held my hand. We talked a little and she enquired if I understood what had been said to me. I asked if I could try the chemotherapy again because I had to make sure the tumour disappeared, as I was getting married in three months, and that I would try anything to stop me being so sick even injections every day!

She again explained it all to me and when she said, "Susan, your body can't do it anymore, so we have to stop some of the treatment!" my response was, "Or what? It will kill me?"

She simply and gently replied "Yes, love!"

I wasn't sure how I was supposed to react or what I was supposed to say, so I didn't do or say anything, I just turned and stared out of the window.

When she left my room, I felt strangely quiet, not upset, not crying - just quiet. I had no feelings of fear, desperation, or panic, just a feeling of warmth and security.

After a few days things started to improve a little. In order to control my sickness they decided to try me with a driver (a small pump) which allowed a measured amount of anti-sickness medication to be absorbed into my blood stream. This was administered by a small butterfly needle in my arm.

Getting to know my new attachment was a nightmare! I couldn't believe it, another needle. However, a new problem – just for a change, was that the needle that sat beneath my skin needed changing every other day due to my arm reacting to the needle and becoming extremely sore around the area and a painful lump forming.

This was not good. However, a wonderful nurse remembered that the children's ward had tubes of cream referred to as 'magic cream' which numbed the skin. When she told me about it, and better still she managed to get me some, I thought all my birthdays had come at once! I was ecstatic to say the least. I soon realised that if I ensured that the magic cream was left on my skin under a patch of cling film for at least twenty minutes to half an hour, it really worked - and woe betide anyone who tried to cut corners!

The cream and the driver with the occasional injection started to make a difference and slowly I began to cope better.

During this stay I was told that my stepfather Steve was also in a ward on the floor below.   He was having another round of chemotherapy due to his cancer causing more problems. I was really pleased - someone to talk to during the day! The nurse gave me permission to visit him, so with my attachment on wheels, I went for a walk. I felt slightly excited and with an almost childlike innocence, I went visiting.

When I arrived on the ward and saw him sitting in a chair at the side of his bed, I was so shocked! My eyes focused only on him, and the others on the ward faded into non-existence.

He looked so ill and I became aware that I felt so scared. I didn't know what to say to him as I walked towards him. I wanted to be positive but I didn't want my positivity to upset him or offend him. I guess that is how people must have felt when they came to visit me or when they saw me.

I bent down and kissed his cheek, and he held my hand. As we sat and chatted I looked into his eyes and listened to how he truly believed I was going to get better. He was excited for me about my wedding and asked me to tell him all about it. I was really pleased as he, my mother and sisters had all said they would love to come to it, and that was just a great blessing. Steve started to tell me that my sister Hannah and her husband Peter had been taking him to their church and that the Pastor, John, and the church congregation had been praying for us both.

I soon realised that Steve had come to know the Lord, and his faith was big and his relationship was a deep and loving one. My fears and my uncomfortable feelings soon melted away, and I no longer saw a desperately ill man, but a man with hope in his eyes and calmness and assurance which made me feel very safe. As I left the ward I turned round to wave and Steve whispered "Susan, trust in the Lord."

Asking for Help

I was so relieved to return home. Every room in the bungalow looked so big and everywhere looked so bright. I was still very poorly and very weak but I was pleased that the new attachment in my arm was working for me most of the time. When it didn't, I agreed to have an injection, but it was great not being sick. However the diarrhoea remained but I coped with it better.

My attachment on my arm had a small oblong devise which looked like a little clutch handbag and had to be carried around. At first this was fine but it became a bit of a nuisance especially during my bath time. It was something of a performance trying to prevent it getting wet, whilst at the same time trying to keep my peg from drowning. So bath times became more of an ordeal.

Poor Ron sometimes couldn't do right for doing wrong during these times. What between trying to interpret my various looks, which became a language of their own, having to have more arms than a octopus to cope with the increasing demands on his co-ordination and problem solving skills, whilst at the same time trying to remain a supportive, caring, sympathetic and patient partner. On more than one occasion I pushed him to the edge and when I did he would look at me and state "Susan when you applied to be my wife, were you the best or were you the only one? cos' I think I've been done!" This would always make me stop and smile. If I ever broke down, which was often during this activity due to feeling so dependent and due to the lack of privacy, he would just say "Come on Susan, you've got to get better for our wedding. Think of Thoresby Hall – it costs too much to cancel it now! I'd never get my money back!"

Because the needle of the attachment needed to be changed and the medication replaced every twenty four hours, it meant that I had to have a district nurse visit every day. The two regular nurses, (my ladies in blue), Lorraine and Lucy were great. Both were very different to each other but both so important to me. Lorraine was a very quietly spoken, gentle and caring woman. This was what I really needed when she first started to visit when I was very poorly. She used to come in and change my medication and my needle when all I could do was just look at her, barely able to talk. I felt very safe in her hands.

Well, Lucy was quite different, but still an amazing nurse. She would almost bounce into the lounge, bubbly although in a sensitive way, always smiling, but when I cried she would be like Lorraine, listen and comfort me. She could make me laugh, especially on the days I was feeling slightly better, especially around negotiating for the time allowed for my magic cream to work.

Sometimes in life you meet people whose job is more than just a job to them. I was so blessed to have these ladies looking after me on a daily basis. When I cried they were caring, when I tried hard to be positive, they were right there with me and encouraged me. As they got to know me my wedding soon became the focus for all the visits, and on the days where I struggled, my ladies in blue would use my wedding to enable me to focus on something positive and keep going.

I started to panic about the wedding and although I had managed to get most important things in place before I started my treatment always the "Miss Organised" I was determined that I would be able to sort out the final preparations myself, but at the time I didn't realise that I would be so ill. Now the time had arrived for the last minute things to start to be arranged and I was faced with the fact that I was too ill to do it. I couldn't expect Ron, as wonderful as he was, to sort it and I don't think he was really bothered about the colour of flowers, favours or invitations.

This was so hard and frustrating for me. I had been looking forward to sorting everything out, what bride doesn't? And I had enjoyed planning everything prior to my treatment, but I knew in my heart, as much as I wanted to, I just couldn't do it. So with cap in hand, I had to ask for help. I needed a team.

My daughters were my first point of contact. Kelly who was pregnant and working agreed to sort out things to keep the young children occupied during the wedding reception, and to gently and lovingly keep me encouraged and 'up' when I was feeling sorry for myself. Paula had more time as she was home looking after my grandson. Like me she was a good organiser which was often interpreted as being bossy, so she was perfect as my link with the wedding and reception venues and for everything else I asked her to do. My shopping partners Michelle and Sharon also came on board, and sorted out bridesmaids' flowers, button holes and my cake. The invitations I requested were terrible and looked like they should be invitations to a funeral, and time was running out.

Maxine amazingly volunteered to make me some new invitations. I was so relieved and it was arranged that I would go to her bungalow in the next village to look though some ideas. This was easier said than done. The first barrier that I had to overcome was my embarrassment about the increasing odour that smothered every room I went into. The second barrier was that I was feeling so ill and weak; I had to fight to stay awake instead of wanting to just to sleep my time away. And thirdly was my on-going difficulty with talking and the state of my hair. Why this would cause me embarrassment I'm not sure, but it did. But the worse thing for me was feeling so helpless and reliant. Even the simple task of making a decision about what I liked and didn't like was difficult. At times I so needed reassurance and support to make simple choices, sometimes my brain felt like it was full of cotton wool and my thoughts were difficult to sort themselves out.

To my relief Maxine listened to what I would like and came up with lots of ideas to help me, and before long I had fabulous invitations. My team of ladies, I have to say were great. When I look back at this time, none of them railroaded me and I continued to be involved and supported. In fact it was a positive experience and one where I feel I was shown again the true meaning of friendship, support and love. Being reliant on others does not mean weakness, I learned its okay to ask and receive help.

In the Eye of Goliath

This was a busy time for everyone; lots of things were happening around me and for my part I had to continue to concentrate on my daily routine, which now included my ladies in blue for practical and emotional support. The stress of my treatment and the effects of it continued to manifest itself as the days went on. The tension between my father, Carole and me became a normal part of my daily routine. Often it wasn't what was said, but what wasn't said, that caused the strain at times or even simple misunderstandings. Looking back at this time, the couple of minor situations that arose resulted in a heightened sensitivity which then led to more misunderstandings and more upset.

At the time I can honestly say, sometimes I wasn't always aware of what was happening around me, and when I did it see it or it involved me, it was like watching a scene that was being played around me although I knew I was being part of it, it was in a very detached way. Often I couldn't organise my thoughts to make sense of anything that happened. It is only now when I look back at this time I can see that there were a lot of signs that my father and Carole were struggling. However, everyone continued with their roles in a quiet way and I saw my father and Carole spend more time away from the bungalow and, when there was any conversation between us, we were all very polite and very controlled.

The effects of the treatment on my body, the emotional state of us all, and my father's fear and inability to remain in control, all contributed to the slow melting away of the family ties that kept us together through this difficult time. Before too long our strained relationships became an accepted and difficult part of my daily routine.

On one of my hospital visits, as usual I was requested to see the dietician, and I knew we had to go through the routine of them trying to increase my intake of liquid food from my one bag of food to two. The problem was I could only manage the one bag, and this would be fed through my peg throughout the night. Any more would cause me to be sick. Despite continuing to try to increase the food over the weeks, I continued to fail, so I always found these visits frustrating. I had discussed this problem with my consultant who agreed that although one bag of food was far from satisfactory, I could just concentrate on the one, but I agreed to ensure that through the day I would use my peg and food pump to replace vital fluid lost because of my diarrhoea. But whenever I visited the dietician, I found myself having to be firm with them in my refusal to the increase, and firm with my explanations. I always felt like they were not listening and often treating me like an awkward child.

At the next weekly check up with my consultant, my father had challenged him – not aggressively, but it was obvious that he wanted a full explanation as to why he had stopped my chemotherapy. When the consultant explained everything, at first this was not enough for my father so he probed a little more. The consultant explained that hopefully I had had enough chemotherapy to help me, but he had little choice but to stop it. Then very respectfully but firmly he informed my father that although he understood my father's concerns, *his* professional concern about my mortality outweighed his need to allay my father's anxiety. My father fell silent and with this we were ushered out of the room.

I could understand why my father felt he wanted to discuss this with the consultant, but on the other hand he knew how ill the chemotherapy had made me, and I had explained what had been discussed with the consultant on the ward. To tell you the truth, I was a little disappointed that my father felt that I could not make an informed decision. Actually I had asked all the questions I needed in order to make the right choice. After all it wasn't really an option, I had no real alternative, quite simply the treatment was killing me!

The Blue Settee

After seeing my consultant, the three of us were once again waiting to see the dietician. As for me it felt as though I was waiting to go into battle. While we were waiting the word "mortality," which had caused my heart to jump and miss a beat as I heard it once again, was swimming around in my inner thoughts and conversations. I began to feel myself becoming increasingly anxious. I felt so weak, so tired and I just didn't want to battle with anyone. I just wanted the dietician to understand that I just could not do what they wanted me to do in increasing my food. My consultant had listened, so today I needed them to.

As I sat next to my father in the large foyer of the treatment area, I turned and looked at him said, "Dad, please don't tell me off about not increasing my food when we go in." As he stood up, Carole said "He only does it because he cares!"

I felt myself just looking into her eyes hoping that she would understand that I desperately didn't want anymore battles. I just couldn't cope with anymore conflict, atmosphere and misunderstandings, I just felt so numb by the word 'mortality' and all I wanted to do was withdraw into myself, to think everything through and place the word into the part of my mind which stores things which I didn't want to face.

I'm not sure how we arrived at the scene that I was faced with and was part of, but it resulted in my father's frustration with me overflowing. I could then be heard informing him that I could not cope with him anymore, being told off, having no privacy and that it all had to stop and, for the remaining two weeks of my treatment, I would make my own arrangements for travelling to the hospital.

It was obvious that all the fear, worries, disappointments and stresses of the last few months were being released. However, no raised voices could be heard, only a somewhat controlled, but emotional and angry exchange from each of us. My father's eyes were clouded with frustration with me, and as he released his emotions he threw down the car keys and walked away, demanding that Carole follow him. Carole refused to go with him thinking this may calm him down but this didn't work.

As we watched him walk up the corridor I felt a sense of relief, although I'm not sure why, as we were now faced with getting home. Carole was not a confident driver so I decided that I would drive home, which given the amount of medication I was on, was perhaps not a good idea, but it had to be done. As we travelled home in silence, I didn't feel upset about what had happened. I felt that I had taken back some of my self-respect and now I had made the decision there was nothing more to be said.

However, the only voice I could still hear ringing in my mind was that of my consultant saying "mortality", it was not the angry hurts that were thrown at me by my father.

My friends stepped in to help Ron get me to the hospital for my treatment, while the atmosphere within the bungalow continued to be strained. Any short conversations between us all were polite, and personal space was respected by everyone. However, my father and Carole appeared to spend a lot more time away from the bungalow. I was also aware there seemed to have been a lot of phone calls and activity while they were around, but then one afternoon my father announced that they were leaving and had found somewhere else to live.

If I was honest I wasn't surprised or upset. I had always had a feeling that one day this would happen, as they had often talked about moving to Wales. At the time though, I wasn't aware that they had already informed Ron about their plans. Ron felt that he had been put in an impossible position by them asking him not to tell me, as he didn't hold with secrets however they were dressed up. But so as not to cause anymore problems Ron kept it to himself, but in the end he had told my father that I needed to be told or else he would tell me himself.

So this is was what my father was now doing, but what I didn't expect was that he was also announcing that he would not be letting me know where they were moving to and that they would not be keeping in touch with me.

As I tried to absorb the words I had heard, I couldn't make sense of his reasons as to why he was doing this, in fact nothing made sense to me. As I listened to all his hurts from as far back as his relationship breakdown with my mother, the loss of his children, his disappointment in me, even right up to the present day, I lay in disbelief and bewilderment. The situation I was now experiencing didn't feel real. I tried to hear what he was saying, but I was having trouble understanding what he was meaning and understanding why. Once again words were hitting a wall of cotton wool within my mind which did not allow me to unpick them and make sense of them.

Later when I thought about the reasons for his decision, I became angry with him. It was okay to move on, but why was he no longer going to be part of my life? Why did every hurt, problem and sacrifice he had made in his life, now feel like there were being laid at my feet?

Throughout the following week, I continued to try to register all his reasons, make sense of and examine the words I had heard. I found myself in the stillness of the nights, fluctuating between blaming myself for everything, trying to recall any misunderstandings or conversations that would account for my father leaving me, and feeling as though this whole situation echoed memories of my childhood. At the same time I could not accept his reasons. In reality I wasn't responsible for his all his hurts past or present, and I wasn't responsible for the fact that my sisters still chose not to have him in their lives. That was between him and them! Furthermore, I couldn't help it if he felt disappointment in me and, above everything else, I couldn't, as much as I tried, recall a situation or anything I did which was bad enough to have caused him to feel this way and to no longer want to be part of my life.

At times I could barely look at him, and when he would come and sit at the end of my bed enquiring in a gentle and caring tone as to how I was, I could not contain my disappointment in him. My father could not understand why I was upset with him. He would not acknowledge that what he was doing was hurtful or that I could not be blamed for everything - every hurt, and every disappointment in his life. But when I challenged this, he would simply turn and walk away in anger. It is difficult trying to talk to someone who has a wall of disappointments in their life.

When I look back at this time, the fact that my father could not cope was not his fault. I think it was too much to expect of him. In truth, what he gave me was a beautiful gift in coming home to help look after me as his child and he did his best. I suppose, in a way, it had been a little naïve of us all to expect that we would cope easily with the stresses and problems that would present to us throughout my journey.

And realistically, the truth is none of us was prepared for the difficult health challenges that we had to face. How could we have been? So, each of us, in our own ways did our best to cope with what we had to face.

Writing about this painful episode in my journey, I was reminded of a story I had heard many times, even from as far back as a child in my Sunday school days. It's funny how it can be the simple stories you hear that often stick in your mind and which speak to you of the different situations you are faced with. God can use them to help you understand situations, to speak to you and even help you gain a sense of peace. The David and Goliath story was just that, as I write about the final breakdown of my relationship with my father. The story shows how a simple faith and belief can triumph over an all consuming fear.

Now I'm not suggesting for one minute that my father was the giant Goliath, although he was scary at times, but my cancer was definitely Goliath, a bigger than life threat and fear which was at times wrapped up in a shroud of anger. This fear and control showed itself throughout my battle; it would often consume everyone and win over the territory of our minds and hearts. David on the other hand had nothing but a simple faith and belief that his God would conquer. He overcame his fear as he stared death in the face. At the lowest times of my battle all I had was a simple faith.

My father's Goliath was fear and control which he could not overcome, so it remained with him and consumed his life to the point that he became unhappy, frightened and ran away both physically and emotionally. We can all do this when we feel we cannot control the situations we are presented with, and I am no exception to this. I remember the sheer devastation of my separation and eventual divorce which had shown me that my Goliath was hurt, fear and anger which was so physically and emotionally painful. It consumed every part of my being and my life, and at the time I just could not find the simple faith of David.

When having little or no control of difficult situations we sometimes find ourselves in, it makes us vulnerable and it is that vulnerability that we find hard, as it opens us up to change. I had had a frightening few months and had stared death in the face. I had no control of anything during this time and my vulnerability was immense, but also this vulnerability allowed my channels of change to be available to God, therefore hanging on to a simple faith and hope.

I'm not saying that like David I truly and wholeheartedly believed that I could overcome my Goliath as David had, but what I had realised was, in my own strength I could not fight my Goliath. I only had a simple faith that God was in my single stone that I could throw at my fear to prevent it becoming painful, consuming and bitter which then gave me a measure of peace.

I wish, with all my heart, that my father could have found his single stone of faith to shoot into the eye of his Goliath and find the strength to overcome and find his peace.

Skies of Victory and Pits of Despair

The two weeks to the end of my treatment were difficult; the effects of the treatment continued to cause me problems. My face, around the area of the treatment from radiotherapy, was very red and had been flaking, although I was fortunate not to be experiencing the problems with my skin breaking and weeping as I had seen other people's faces were doing. The infection in my mouth continued and the smell still caused me embarrassment. In addition to the excessive amount of phlegm continuing to run down my throat came the added problem of a dry mouth. On top of everything else the diarrhoea was still taking its toll on me which resulted in another hospital stay, in the same small room.

Once again I lay staring out of the window for hours, my thoughts still trying to make sense of my father's announcement and the disappointment I felt. I had my mother and sisters back in my life, my family had begun to feel as though it could be complete and 'normal' but just as I thought I had it all, I was to lose my father. I had been so excited by the fact that "all" my family were to be present at my wedding, all the hurt from the past was to be put to one side for my day and my father was to give me away, but now that was not to happen. So by gaining my family, I lost my family.

However, in the end I had to resign myself to just accepting this situation, as the alternative would be constant anger which could easily turn into bitterness. I knew how bitterness could destroy any chance of forgiveness or moving on with my life. I had seen this at times from both my parents, so I felt that the best thing I could do was let my father go and do what he felt was right for him. This was extremely difficult as I felt let down by him, but the alternative would have prevented me from moving on with my life and I had to trust and leave it with God. Again I had no control of this situation.

After a couple of days I returned home to my final days of my daily routine with my friends helping me. Everyday I had crossed out the treatment dates on my list, and then the day arrived when I was so relieved I got to thirty five! The radiotherapists shared in my excitement on my last visit. They had seen my struggles at various stages of my illness and treatment as I fought to continue to walk into each session. Sometimes it was only with their help could I lift myself onto the treatment bed. I could not speak to thank them only say it with a grateful smile.

It was an absolutely fantastic feeling. I had done it! I had made it! Although as the dust settled, I was disappointed that my health would only improve slowly. The hospital had informed me that the effects of the treatment continued for a further two weeks after everything stopped. It was only then when it had peaked that I would slowly begin to feel a little better. But the wedding was now only eight weeks away and I wanted to get better much quicker. I didn't want to be ill or look ill on my wedding day, we had worked so hard to get through everything and we wanted our day to be perfect.

The day after my final radiotherapy session I received a call at home from my consultant. He informed me that, due to the research programme, I was to have a further ten radiotherapy treatments. As I listened to him speaking to me on the phone, my excitement at finishing the treatment came crashing down around me. I could not believe what I was hearing and although I could understand the reasons and agreed with them, I was totally devastated. I felt we had strived so hard for this day and now we had to start all over again. I wasn't sure if I had the ability to cope with it emotionally or physically. Two weeks felt like a life time.

The effects of the extra radiotherapy sessions caused me to become excessively tired again, and the lack of energy and discomfort in my mouth became more difficult to cope with, resulting in more medication being needed.

The Blue Settee

I found myself very low and found it extremely difficult to be positive and prevent myself from becoming more withdrawn from everything and everyone, including Ron. I felt I didn't have enough physical or emotional energy left in me to fight. I wasn't sure where my strength and determination to get through these extra sessions were to come from because I was so low. Ron was supportive and did his best as usual, so with almost robot like behaviour I returned to my daily routine.

Carole had informed my father about the two extra weeks of treatment I needed, but he simply said I had to do it and that I didn't really have a choice. My father and Carole continued to be busy so I didn't really see much of him, nor did I want to, and to be honest, I just couldn't cope at the time with the emotional baggage that came with him.

My Macmillan nurse, Angela arrived to see me. In all the upset I had forgotten she was coming. On her previous visits I had been positive and thankful that I was managing to get through the treatments. She had been great, getting information for me to help me understand various parts of my treatment and give advice about things to help me on a day to day basis.

But during this visit I felt that I just couldn't cope. We chatted about my feelings, about my cancer, my father and the situation, and before too long I found myself crying. My heart felt so heavy and full of tears and I felt so lost in my hurt. All the anger, upset and despair just seemed to overflow before me. I hadn't cried like this before and I thought I would never stop.

I could not understand - why couldn't I cope? I was nearly at the end of my treatment and I so wanted to feel better. I was getting married soon and had so much to look forward to. Angela sat and listened as I laid everything before her. When my crying paused a little, she simply asked me if I realised how ill I had been, how much I had been through and reminded me that it was hard for anyone who has had to face their own death. She said I should not be surprised I was feeling like that, it was a normal reaction.

As I heard this, I took a sharp intake of breath and released my tears with even more emotions from the anguish of the last few months - the fears, the sleepless nights, my sickness, my father and my utter despair which were all so painfully routed within them. The physical pain of my tears rising from my inner self felt as though they were squeezing the life out of my heart and were now being thrust into a raging waterfall of emotions and landing at the feet of Angela.

Angela gave me time to cry and sat and comforted me. When my crying eventually softened, I stated that I knew that I should be grateful I was alive, but I just could not believe what had happened to me. I then found myself telling her that I was a Christian and that I should know better.

As I blurted out some of the stories between my uncontrolled sobbing, my eyes streaming with tears and my very sticky mouth from the lack of saliva, which caused my words to be muffled and inaudible at times, I told her of how God had 'shown up' throughout the last few months during the lowest times in my journey.

As I presented her with this rather mixed up and hurried snapshot of the last few months, I was not even sure if what I was saying even made any sense. I just felt that I needed to quickly get it off my chest in the hope that it would convince her that I was being an ungrateful Christian after God had clearly been with me.

After my hasty presentation, I was sobbing with my head nestled in my hands and my eyes hung down in shame at my feelings. But before I could say anymore she gently informed me that she too was a born again Christian and that what I had said had shown her that God had been there for me throughout my journey, but it was alright to be upset and cry and that she knew that God understood how I was feeling.

We sat together and chatted about all the wonderful ways in which God had let me know he was with me through the dark times, and how He had carried me when I needed carrying, comforted me when I needed comforting and gave me the strength to carry on when I had no strength.

This was a special time for me; my anguish and despair lifted and was replaced with an overwhelming feeling of joy and amazement at the wonders of God. I realised I had experienced the true meaning of a faithful and loving Father. I had been through a difficult battle and God would understand that. As Angela left my home she asked me to remember to continue to Trust in God with all my heart as He would never let me down.

Fish & Chips

My final radiotherapy session was a bit of an anti-climax. I was just so relieved to get to the end of it all and then to concentrate on getting stronger for my wedding.

The hospital was right. I didn't start to see any improvement for weeks. I continued on morphine and everything else I could have, but my sense of 'I've made it' remained with me and having our wedding to look forward to helped with the difficult atmosphere within the bungalow.

Slowly I began to see things being taken out of the bungalow or packed into boxes. It was a strange situation. If anybody had been looking in on it, they would have seen everything as being normal, but it was far from normal and it felt impossible at times.

Ron decided that we should go away for a couple of days over the weekend, not too far, just to the local coast. I really enjoyed the drive there, everything looked so alive and interesting and I remember thinking that my world felt so much bigger and amazing, so I didn't want to miss anything.

The hotel was cosy and comfortable and overlooked the sea. It had been years since I had visited this part of the coast and I was fascinated to see all the wind turbines in the sea - although I wasn't sure what I thought of them as they appeared to dominate the scenery, but nevertheless, I was just relieved to be somewhere else other than the bungalow or the hospital.

We wrapped up well and went for short walks, sometimes in silence, each of us lost in our own thoughts - sometimes we just chatted about nothing in particular. I think we were both keen not to let our conversations throughout the weekend be ruled by the last few months or the situation with my father.

I have always found that fish and chips taste better at the seaside and, during this weekend break; they smelt wonderful as we walked past the shops. We decided that we would find somewhere we could sit down and Ron could "partake in a little pleasure", as he put it. As we walked past a fish shop I noticed a sign with an offer. Knowing how much Ron likes offers, I proudly proclaimed I could save him some money! This stopped him in his tracks and I could see him examining and analysing the offer. Then with an indignant tone in his voice, he calmly called me a 'cheeky chuff' and then went on to say that this offer was no good - he wasn't that old, how could I even think he was that old and then started to walk away.

I was not having this and calmly and stubbornly remained routed to my spot. I had found him an offer to save him some money, and come what may he was going to see that. So I again pointed out the sign and stated that the offer was for over fifty fives and I was sure he was fifty seven. I then watched him in amazement as he read it out aloud a few times, while I stood listening to him in fits of laughter. I'm not sure why he read it out loud; perhaps he thought I had changed it.

As I watched him eat his special offer, I continued to chuckle. It was good to feel normal for a while, well as normal as we could be when I still had to have a sleep in the afternoon and use my peg for food and water, but it did not seem to matter this weekend.

The evening before we went home, we went for a final walk by the sea and eventually found a sheltered seat in an enclosed garden full of spring flowers; it was such a beautiful sight. As we huddled together on the seat, it felt like we were the only two people in the world and as we sat taking in the beauty we began to talk about the last few months. Sitting in this little piece of paradise, January felt like a lifetime away, not a few months ago. So much had happened; we could not believe what we had been through and now we had to look at picking up the pieces of our lives and start to place them together to start to live again.

The Blue Settee

As we sat we had so many questions, how were we to start living again, would our lives ever feel normal again, would cancer always dominate it, could we find a new life together after putting our future on hold? We didn't answer any of the questions and I don't think we expected to, to be truthful, but it was enough for us to just be honest, say it and face it. The answers didn't appear to be important to us; it was enough to acknowledge our feelings.

I then found myself asking Ron if he thought he could be a husband rather than a carer. He was a brilliant carer but I wanted a husband now. I'm not sure why or what exactly I really meant by this but, I think I was worried because I wanted to feel 'normal' again and be in a 'normal' relationship again.

Ron just laughed at me and said that when I applied to be his wife, he forgot to read the fine print of my application, but he wasn't too worried though, he just couldn't wait for me to look after him when we were married. He then informed me he would have to train me up to his standards! We both laughed at this prospect, as I'm not the best nurse or housewife, but I promised to do my best.

All I really wanted was to just lead a normal life again, laugh at the daftest things, get mad at the daftest things and cry at the daftest things.

As we travelled home I felt so uplifted by the rest. We had even managed to talk about our wedding and we were both excited about all the things we had planned. The wedding was soon to be with us.

Steve

After arriving home we entered the bungalow but it felt strangely empty, not by the lack of furniture, as all my things were around, but just empty. Everything in my father's room had gone.

On the breakfast bar was a letter addressed to me. The contents were not particularly positive, but it had my father's final thoughts which were obviously important to him, and ensured that he had the last say with regard to our father and daughter relationship, which had sadly come to the end of the line.

I tried not get too upset by the letter. I had come to terms with his decision well before he left, although I think it was very sad but it appeared from the letter that was the way he wanted it. Ron encouraged me to carry on and not to focus on it, and as for me, I felt I had spent enough time crying and regretting the way the relationship had broken down and now I needed to try to move on. So I pushed it to the back of my mind and tried to forget about it all - for a while.

Plans for the wedding were definitely on the way. This gave both Ron and I lots to concentrate on, which also gave us a welcome break from the effects of my treatment.

I had visited my mother and stepfather Steve, and had asked him if he would give me away. Fortunately neither of them enquired why or what had happened with my father, which was a relief. How do you tell people that your father had moved away and you do not know where to?

My family were all excited about the wedding. As much as it was a distraction for us to look forward to something so positive, I think it also helped *them* by taking the focus away from the situation they were all faced with - Steve's battle with cancer.

I had cancelled my father's wedding suit and Steve had been for his fitting. I hadn't been aware of how ill he had become until I was told how he struggled to get up the steps into the shop, but he had been determined to do it, to be there for me on my wedding day.

A few weeks later Steve's health deteriorated and my mother asked me to visit him in the hospital. When I arrived on the ward; I was so taken back when I saw him. Steve was slumped on the side of his bed; his body was now totally broken.

My mother talked about how she and Steve had undertaken what would be a last visit to the borders of Scotland the week before, and had stayed in a hotel as they had often done in the past for a short break. On previous visits they had bought each of my sisters a necklace and this time they went back to get me one.

As my mother continued to chat to Ron and me, Steve had a brief moment where he became aware of who was with him. With his eyes full of love, he signalled for me to sit next to him on the bed. As I sat with him, he stretched out his hand and placed a small box in mine. When I opened it, he whispered to me that he had been back to Gretna to buy me the necklace to be the same as my sisters.

I was taken aback by this as it was unexpected, but then he held my hand again, pulled me close to him and then whispered in my ear, "I love you Susan", and then said "I know I didn't do right by you and I'm so sorry, I should have been there for you". I was surprised by what he said, so I squeezed his hand, kissed him on his cheek and told him that I was also sorry and that I loved him. With that, his moment passed. This was the last time Steve spoke to me.

Within a couple of days the Macmillan nurse got him into the hospice and before too long we were being told that his time with us was coming to an end.

I have found myself struggling to write about this part of my journey, as I am faced, as I look back, with a mixture of emotions, from feeling extreme and deep sadness with the death of Steve, to a thankfulness and relief that he found the meaning of life itself.

How do you start to record someone's final journey which is a very private and personal time, whilst at the same time preserving the dignity of everyone involved and include a picture of a family coming together? If I am honest I have tried for many weeks to think through what I felt I needed or wanted to say. Part of my difficulty has been that while recalling and reliving some of my precious memories, I found it more painful than when I went through it.

At the time, I had very little emotional strength and looking back I realise that God must have been shielding me from the full trauma of what was happening, because it is only in hindsight that I realise how deep my feelings went. In a way, looking back has helped me go through the grieving process and allowed me to feel some of the anguish that my family bravely went through.

However, I would like to try and give a little insight into a beautiful and precious moment in the history of a united family - 'my family', which was brought together by a tragedy. But as I start to write this insight and face some of my feelings, it has become apparent that it is my time to grieve the loss of my gentle giant.

Picking up the telephone and delivering the news to Kelly and Paula was made easier by the fact that we all knew in our hearts that Steve's journey was to finish soon and the beginning of a new one was about to start.

Kelly and Adrian travelled from the Midlands with Emmy to visit him with the hope that he may see the granddaughter he had never had chance to meet. They arrived at the bungalow following their visit and were pleased that they had chance to spend a few precious moments with him where he had managed to open his eyes to see Emmy, smiled and closed them again.

Later Ron, Paula and I had visited. I felt so relieved; he looked so comfortable and peaceful. You could have easily been encouraged as to how well he looked; you could have even thought he would get better again. I found that my mother was coping remarkably well and relieved that he was now more comfortable in the hospice.

The call that everyone dreads, but knows will happen one day came, and despite the fact that it was expected, it still brought a feeling of panic and dread of what was to come. I don't think you can be really prepared for the death of a loved one as there is always a painful rollercoaster ride through a grey and heavy cloud of disbelief.

When Ron, I and the girls arrived at the hospice we were met with a lovely calm atmosphere. I was expecting to be met with a tidal wave and an outward pouring of feelings, emotions and despair by everyone. But what I found were my mother, sisters Hannah, Avril, Penny and my niece Laura sitting in small room with Steve, and although they were visibly upset, they were comforting each other in an ambience of love, dignity and affection, which was befitting for a man who lived for his family.

Time with Steve felt as though it became a precious jewel in the crown of Hope and as a family we travelled through the many special moments of Steve's final journey that would then be a treasured and priceless gift for each of us.

Pastor John arrived to support us and be with Steve through this time. His presence was reassuring and his kind and gentle nature was very comforting. It just seemed the natural thing for him to be with us - it wasn't intrusive, it just felt right that he should share this time with us even though my mother and two of my sisters did not go to church.

With Steve's favourite worship songs gently playing in the background, sitting around him we each went through a mixture of emotions and shared our own private memories with each other. We cried together and we laughed together as a family, each of us celebrating his life and going through the process of letting him go.

I remember thinking what an amazing memory we were creating when we were all sat enjoying my mother's many stories about their 'quirky' life together which were so funny. I recall my utter astonishment when looking at everybody including myself and Pastor John, laughing so much at the picture my mother was painting of their romantic vow to ensure they ended their life together as old 'folk' with their favourite bottle of whisky.

With puzzled looks on our faces as we were all trying to see the romantic picture my mother was painting, which was not how we would have described them as a couple. My mother then proudly announced that she would not have gone through with it because she knew Steve would make sure she went first so he could have polished off his favourite whisky without her, and she was having none of that!

A little time later we found ourselves laughing again, but at my mother's expense. You see it came to light that she has a real aversion to green peas. I remember feeling shocked about this. I didn't know that my mother couldn't stand to look at these green things that roll around a plate. How bizarre! But it didn't really matter, we just seemed to need to laugh together and recall many things and events that made up this once disjointed family. As I listened to my mother and sisters bring stories into this special time, it felt that Steve was very much part of the celebration of his family. All the laughter, as well as the quiet times, and the tears felt so important and was a natural process for us to go through, but it was a togetherness I had not experienced for a long time with my mother and sisters.

After one of our moments of relief and celebration, which appeared to lift us all and give us a small measure of strength, without realising it I found myself detached from the conversations in the room. It suddenly struck me that I 'really, really' didn't know my mother had an aversion to peas, but then there was so much I didn't know about my mother and what they were all really like as a family - although I could see that my mother, Avril and Penny, who is my half-sister and sixteen years my junior, were all very close.

The Blue Settee

In a way I guess the best way to describe the way I had always seen our family was one of two halves. There was Avril and Penny and their children, and then there was Hannah and me and our children. Quite when and how this divide happened I'm not sure, but this had become the accepted "norm" for our family life over the years. I would look at Avril and Penny's relationship with my mother and Steve and feel somewhat on the outside, and in some ways I suppose this detachment had made it easy for me to cut ties with them in the past.

Steve was the lynch-pin of his family, and he had been the one who had ensured that Avril and Penny were taken care of, especially when they went through troubled times. So when Steve was no longer able to do this, the void had to be filled. Hannah and Peter had stepped into that role, working hard to ensure that everyone was looked after. Because of this, Hannah, Peter and her children had recently been experiencing a little more closeness with the rest of the family than I had been, but up to that point it had been the normal 'make up' of our family to see me and my sister Hannah and our children be on the peripheral of their closeness.

However, as I looked at the scene of love and laughter being played before me, it wasn't bitterness or sadness I felt at the lack of shared experiences and memories, but with a dawning realisation that there are seasons in our lives.

You see, when Steve came into my life I had no trust of men, or very little trust in anyone to be honest. My parents' acrimonious marriage, separation and eventual divorce, in addition to having been abused, had left me emotionally fragile but with a hard and untrusting character. In time I realised Steve just wanted to make me, my sisters Hannah and Avril and my mother safe, happy and loved. And that was what I had really needed as a child.

While laughing, listening and watching my family together I knew that Steve had been in my life for a reason. I needed to learn to trust again as a child, therefore he actually gave me a beautiful gift and a priceless and precious memory.

As I continued to sit, looking in on this scene, lost in my own thoughts, I experienced a reality 'moment'. As lovely as it was to experience the closeness of my family, was it real? What would the future hold for me, my children or even my sister Hannah and her children? Did I have enough space in my life to include my family and their needs now Steve was not looking after them? I hadn't been used to doing simple things like ringing my mother regularly, having to think about supporting my sisters, doing family 'things' beyond my own daughters and husband? Did I even want it to change? It all felt slightly surreal and a little bit alien to me.

As I slowly looked around at each of my sisters and my mother, I wondered if I could even be the eldest daughter and the older sister? Was it a role I wanted in the future? The words 'my family' to me and my sister Hannah had always meant being my mother's 'other family', so could it even change and move on for any of us? Could I dare take the chance to be hurt again? Everyone's heard the phrase 'honour thy father and thy mother' but to be truthful I wasn't sure if I could do that or if I even really understood what that meant for me in the future.

For most of the time my health had faded into the background. I had fought my feelings of being unwell for a little while - I didn't want to make a fuss or moan, and I didn't want to upset my family or alarm Ron. But with Ron and Pastor John's insistence, I gave in, took my medication and quietly retired to the allocated room.

Hardly daring to close my eyes I lay in the dark. Although conscious of my surroundings, I hadn't become aware that the reality of what was happening around me had slowly begun to raise up in me a flood of emotions that overwhelmed my determination to hold myself together.

As this massive surge of emotion flooded into the room, I found that my tears of despair for Steve were now being shed for me. I was so thankful and so relieved that I had survived, that it wasn't me in the room with my children and husband-to-be sharing memories. These thoughts were soon to be intertwined again with my disbelief and horror that I had been through this type of journey in the first place. As the fullness of the flood continued to engulf me, I started to panic almost losing control, what about my wedding? We had worked so hard to get there, what was I to do now Steve wasn't going to be able to give me away? I felt suffocated with panic and conflicting emotions and I knew I needed to get hold of myself before losing it completely.

Sitting up and turning on the bedside lamp I took a deep breath and tried to work out what exactly I was feeling and why. In my imagination I had created a perfect picture of my wedding with my father giving me away, and with Steve and my mother smiling at us in the background. Then the picture had been repainted with my father's abrupt departure from my life and I had just begun to get used to a new image, one of me walking down the aisle on Steve's arm. I had imagined us both feeling victorious on my special day, both having faced death and both of us having beaten it. But now that dream was being shattered in the next room. I felt as though all my dreams were destined to be broken. And in that moment I knew such despair and fear. I felt like I had come full circle - my father had left me again as he had done when I was a little girl and now Steve was leaving too and for a moment I felt strangely very alone.

As I left the room, to tell you the truth I felt a little ashamed of myself. How could I have been so selfish and so self-absorbed? But, while pulling myself together to return to my family, I knew that I needed to put them first and be there for them, even though I wasn't sure I could do it. I was frightened in case my tears once again would be for me and not for Steve. But as I slowly walked towards the door I felt as though I was walking through a crowd to fight my way to the room, while all the time asking myself if I could face this final farewell? With my heart thumping and my eyes fighting to ensure they held onto their tears, I heard the silent whisper in my ear 'Trust in the Lord Susan'. When I entered the room my daughter Kelly was gently singing Steve's favourite song, "Be Still, for the presence of the Lord." There was something special in that song that touched me instantly; there was a wonderful presence, calmness, peace and love in the room, something that totally dissolved my fears.

I took my place with my sisters and my mother, and as I sat and listened to the song playing in the background, I became aware of how gentle the words were. They appeared to match the tenderness that was being displayed by my mother towards her husband. All the fight and anguish of the year could no longer be seen rooted in the character of her face. She had a gentleness and softness that brought back the beauty of her younger years into the silent memories she was privately reliving with every stroke of Steve's brow. She was once again the beautiful woman that was seen in the eyes of her husband.

As my eyes slowly focused on my sisters Avril and Penny, I could see that they were each trying to be so strong for Steve. As I watched them, I didn't see two frightened children without their father, but two brave and dignified women shedding their tears for the strong, caring and gentle rock in their lives. They had been with their father every step of the way in his painful journey and they were with him now, strong, dedicated, and their support to him and our mother was as it had always had been, unwavering and constant.

Then I looked to Hannah and Peter and I realised how tired they were. They had fought tirelessly for Steve and the family, running backwards and forwards to hospital, running my mother around, they had been totally absorbed in the fight for him and everyone else, ensuring that everyone was taken care of, physically, emotionally, practically, spiritually. It felt to me, as I looked at them, as though they had been in a relay race, running hard on behalf of Steve, baton in their hand, but now the time had come to pass the baton on; they were having to fight an inner battle to let go. They had beseeched heaven relentlessly on his behalf, but God was calling him home, it was time for them to pass the baton on and they were coming to the end of their own battle. I knew how hard this was for them, how tired they were, and how sad that very soon it would all be over.

I have beautiful memories of Steve's grandchildren lovingly saying goodbye. There was a gentle dignity in all of them, each supporting each other and showing affection towards my mother. Whereas as children they had been so strongly upheld by their grandmother, the roles had now reversed. Now they were young adults, each supporting her as she had once supported them.

In the bible it talks about branches being grafted back onto a tree, and for years it felt like I was a broken branch that had somehow become detached from the rest of the tree – the rest of the family. But in those special moments before Steve's passing, I felt that something wonderful and amazing and miraculous had happened. Somehow I had been picked up and grafted back onto the tree, the family tree. Somehow I felt I belonged again. And the tree had been made whole again.

The final picture I remember was my mother holding Steve's hand and all the family sitting quietly around the bed. Steve's breathing had become shallow. My mother was stroking his forehead; she leant over, kissed his cheek and said softly, "We're all here together Steve, and we're all ok, so it's alright for you to leave now!"

The Chiming of the Clock

Pulling up to the gates of the church we were met by a few people who were waiting to see my mother and sisters and give support and comfort to them before they walked with Steve into the church. During the hustle and bustle of the moment, I was taking in the sights around me.

You see this was the church where my first marriage had taken place. It was the place where all my dreams had been blessed thirty years ago, and apart from attending my sister's wedding many years ago, before today I hadn't been back. It was very strange returning but nothing seemed to have changed.

After taking my place in the family procession behind Steve, I looked up at the church tower clock and as we slowly walked towards it, it chimed. I was reminded about the last time I walked towards the clock. I had been holding Steve's arm, he had been so proud of me. I could hear him saying to me "Are you ready for this Aggie" (Steve's nickname for all his girls) as we waited for the signal to enter the church to the wedding march. As the clock struck 4 o'clock, Steve and I had begun the slow walk towards my hopes and dreams, all of which were wrapped up in my smiles and excitement about my new life with my childhood sweetheart and the man of my dreams.

But this time the walk was different. With my arm now holding onto Ron, we joined the slow and silent procession as it ambled purposefully towards the big oak door. Walking almost in time with the chime of the clock announcing our presence, I became conscious of how my life had changed beyond all recognition. All my youthful notions, my expectations of life, some of which naturally melted away with my maturity, and others, I suppose, disappeared through the battles and hurts of life…

As we entered through the large wooden door it was my turn to say "Are we ready for this Steve?" and as we walked into the dim light of church I was met by a sea of tear soaked faces from a church full of people who cared for him. I recall that I was taken aback by this, although I shouldn't have been as Steve was a local lad who did well and everyone knew him. But again I suppose I had not been a part of his life for some time, and you very often don't think of the wider life that a person has until you are faced with something like a funeral, then you begin to see what an impact we can have on our colleagues, friends and family.

Funerals can be strange things. They can be full of the celebration of the person's life or almost a process that has to be completed. Fortunately Steve's was a celebration and having Pastor John leading this time brought something of the real Steve, the husband, father, stepfather, granddad, friend and colleague into this time for sharing memories, giving comfort and hope to all and showing us Steve's understanding and belief that he was leaving us for somewhere better.

To be honest, as I write this passage one year on, I really can't remember much about the exact message of the service, except that both Pastor John and my sister Hannah spoke and both of them used some of the writings from a book Steve was reading which he had underlined. But I do recall the message was encouraging and comforting and we were very aware that Steve wanted to say something to us all. As for me, I continued to be part of the celebration, listening to the words but at the same time drifting in and out of my own thoughts. I remember sitting listening to Pastor John talk, but; my eyes were on the flowers draped over Steve's coffin. I can't even recall what colour or what flowers they were, but as I continued to focus on them, I realised that Steve wanted to share something of his Hope with his friends and family - even after he had left us.

As I sat, I wondered what people who knew Steve thought of his faith and his Hope and, if I were them, what I would be feeling if I didn't have Hope. Before I realised it, with my eyes continuing to be fixed on the flowers, I even questioned my own belief. Had it become stronger because I had been faced with death, as Steve had, and was I just clinging onto a hope that there was something after death?

It has always been accepted that when people become ill, they sometimes find religion a helpful support and, in a sense, other people allow them this comfort – tolerating it much more than at other times. But was my experience of feeling that God was and had been with me been simply that? Had I just been 'clinging on' to something? Was God simply 'my crutch'?

I had a genuine sense of reality that despite everything and the struggle to survive, I was sitting in this church alive and looking at a new future because God had been with me in my journey.

And just as God had been with me throughout my journey, it was clear that He had also been with Steve throughout his. And the message that Steve wanted his family to hear during that funeral service was that God had been his Hope, even to the end, but it was not until much later, as I prepared to write this book, that I became fully aware of how God had been preparing and comforting Steve in his final months.

In preparation for writing about Steve, Hannah had given me the book which she had given him for his birthday in January. The book is a daily reading one with thoughts and scriptures for morning and evening by C.H. Spurgeon.

Looking in the book and reading the words underlined by Steve, I became very aware that this was a special and intimate time that Steve had been sharing with God. Clearly God had been so close to Steve during this time.

At the beginning of the book Steve had written "Hope and Faith" and this certainly was what God had given him.

As I read some of his thoughts through the weeks and days before he left us, the words that Steve had underlined showed a man at peace.

The underlined quotes showed clearly how God had spoken to Steve in his time of need, and reminded me of how God in different ways had also revealed himself to *me* in *my* time of need. God had been speaking to us both, but in ways that were totally different and individual, words that were personal to each of us – words that took into account our unique needs.

*Morning thought of the day - March 13*th - Steve highlighted*: "we would assure you, as from the Lord that if you seek Him He will be found of you, Jesus casts out none who come to Him. You shall not perish if you trust Him" (2Kings)*

*Evening thought of the day – March 13*th - *"Noah has been looking out for his dove all day long and is ready to receive her, she just had the strength to reach the edge of the ark, she can hardly alight upon it, and is ready to drop when Noah puts forth his hand and pulls her in unto him" (Genesis 8:9)*

Steve had experienced God's love a number of years ago but had drifted away and, as for me, I too had experienced God's love and although I had been seeking Him, the hurts, disappointments and lack of trust had hardened my heart not allowing anyone to really get near me, not my family and not even God.

The dove, in the underlined passage, had been wandering looking for land - she had flown as far as she could and returned unsuccessful, desperately weary, desperately fearful, but Noah just stretched out his hand and pulled her in.

Both Steve and I had fought our battles, both had been weary and fearful; we had both experienced the feeling of our journey coming to the end. God didn't turn round and chastise us for wandering away; He opened His hand and pulled us into Him. For Steve He brought him home, and for me He gave me a Hope and a Peace, something I hadn't truly experienced before.

Steve's final thoughts -

March 18th - *"His love for thee will never cease. Rest in confidence that even down to the grave Christ will go with you, and up from it He will be your guide to the celestial hills" (John 15:9)*

March 21st *–"Lord end my winter, and let my spring begin".*

My gentle giant left us to be with his Father on the 2nd April - Good Friday.

Chicken Drumsticks

The countdown was well on the way for my wedding day. The difficulties with infections in my mouth, eating and feeling tired didn't seem to matter. My team of ladies were all busy with the final preparations for the big day. I enjoyed sitting and playing with the ribbons and wrapping up all the presents, making things pretty and being a bit creative was something I used to love to do.

Even so, the day drawing ever nearer seemed to take its time arriving and this just made the sense of excitement even more strong. I guess you would liken it to waiting and counting down to your holiday - before you realise it, all the wishing and dreaming becomes a reality.

What now seemed a life time away, was the initial excitement about getting married that I had experienced before my diagnosis. Back then I had embarked on the usual 'girlie' thing and begun to look for ideas for a wedding dress. I had had a bee in my bonnet about not wanting to look like 'mutton dressed as lamb', so with my usual determination I had embarked on my mission to find my 'wow!' dress. My first port of call was the internet, so with loads of confidence I typed - "wedding dresses for mature brides". Waiting patiently and full of excitement, I was soon to be stunned into disbelief! You see the response to what I thought was a reasonable and sensible request produced pictures of Camilla in her wedding attire with Prince Charles. I wasn't that "mature!" Disappointment was an understatement but before too long I found my 'wow!'

Standing patiently behind the curtain in the cubical which had been reserved for me, I was a little nervous. A few weeks before, with both daughters accompanying me, I had tried on my dream dress, but I have to be honest it was no longer the 'wow!' I thought it would be. When I looked in the mirror it didn't fit like it had months before, in fact as much as my 'ladies in waiting' were trying to help me see how lovely it could look, it just didn't work. But they assured me that it would be the dress I longed for by my final visit.

Waiting for my final 'fitting' visit seemed to drag and resulted in me becoming more worried about everything; not just my dress, but also about the lumps on my arms from the needles which had connected me to my medication.

I was convinced these lumps would be the focus of everyone and that's all people would see and then if that wasn't enough, on top of everything else, how would I cope with everyone seeing the marks on my face and neck?

These marks showed the outline of where my mask had been when I was given the radiotherapy. The result was visible marks which looked like a dark tan running across my cheeks and down the side of my neck leaving a clear pale pathway running up the middle of my neck and face.

I tried lots of different methods to cover it up, various foundations – some of which made me have the skin tone of a Jamaican, others that made me look like a clown, and I began to feel quite frantic about it - the marks becoming an obsession that was stealing all the joy out of me for my big day.

It was the stern reproach of a good friend that finally brought me back down to earth and put it all in perspective. She put it to me that the people who were at the wedding would be the ones who had been with me through my battle with cancer and that actually they would not be looking at my scars, but rejoicing in the fact that I had made it to this day at all. That perhaps I should see my marks as not so much a distraction but as battle scars which I should be proud of.

The final issue that came to light was the issue of my peg. It was not so much a vanity issue, as a practical one. Under my dress, which was designed to be fitted perfectly, was a rather conspicuous bulge, giving me, as I thought, the appearance of having a third nipple. With hindsight, I guess I could have gotten away with it and as others suggested my flowers strategically held could have disguised it – but as with other things, I wasn't full of grace about it, and yet another bee appeared in my bonnet which needed to be sorted.

After a bit of battling with the dietician who was not convinced that the peg should be removed, I enlisted the support of my GP and consultant and within two days was sitting in a room to have the peg removed.

Once again I was stunned into disbelief that there was to be no anaesthetic for this procedure. I had been fully expecting to be knocked unconscious for it, but no! It was simply going to be a case of one two three and away we go! I had visions of a massive balloon in my stomach being yanked out of a pin hole (which obviously was an exaggerated version of how it was) but in reality, when it came to it, it was rather like whipping off a plaster and then my own hand being slapped over it to apply pressure to the new, small wound.

Nonetheless, even having been assured that after ten minutes I could leave, my brain could not seem to accept that my entire stomach contents would not fall through the hole I imagined had been left by the removal of the peg! I lay frozen in the moment, hardly daring to move, my hand clasped in shocked horror over the place where the peg had once been, staring at the clock as the hands moved round.

An hour and ten minutes later the nurse was very surprised to see me there when she popped her head round the door. She very calmly and nicely told me that I could go home and that nothing would seep out, but I could see her inner laughter in her eyes and I knew that she would be telling her colleagues when she returned to the nurses' station.

I walked out of the hospital as I had done the day the peg was first put in on Christmas Eve, bent double, clutching my stomach like a pregnant woman. Even in my car, I could not quite believe that my stomach contents were safely tucked away, and pressed a cushion tightly against it, just in case....

To my relief my final fitting arrived and I found myself in the familiar little cubical waiting nervously, when my ladies in waiting announced that the dress was ready. However, there had to be a couple of adjustments. My daughter Paula, at an earlier visit, had introduced me to the wonderful invention - a must for every woman - 'chicken fillets' - so with my new found cleavage and everything either pushed up or tucked in, I was dressed and escorted into the lovely bright room and placed in front of the large mirrored wall.

As I gazed into the mirror the sounds of gasps from my sister Hannah and the ladies in waiting filled the room. But as for me I remained silent. Unfortunately this was being interpreted by everyone as me being unhappy with my dress, but this was not the case. When I looked into the mirror what I saw was someone who looked so different. Every woman wants to look like the princess she dreamt of as a child in a beautiful Cinderella dress, but I have to be honest, yes I loved my dress but what I saw was someone I didn't really recognise.

Swaying from side to side, I could see that the person looked so tiny. If this was me what had happened to my body? Where had it gone? I couldn't get over my face. I had always boasted and had indeed been so proud about my lack of winkles, but now all I could see was a little face with large crevices marking the outline of a mouth and forehead and crows feet that looked like a flock of birds had danced all over it.

As I strained to look closer at the image in the mirror I didn't really know the person I was seeing. Scanning the reflection with a growing sense of urgency, trying to make sense of what and who I was seeing, trying desperately to appear pleased, I realised that the ladies and Hannah were clearly amazed at what they were seeing.

I soon began to relax and did the 'little girl' twirling thing, enjoying the attention, laughing and enjoying every moment of feeling pretty and a princess. After a couple of minutes my laughing soon trickled away. I became overwhelmed by the sense of reality that I had made it! I was actually stood with my wedding dress, a week before I was to get married and I really was going to make it!

As tears slowly fell down my face I looked at Hannah. She and my ladies in waiting were obviously feeling my sense of relief and were also sharing my emotions. It was a very special moment. I left my final fitting full of excitement and very grateful for chicken fillets.

Over the next few days my excitement remained and for a brief moment my health over the past few months faded into a memory box which was hidden under a blanket of relief and normality. I could hardly contain my excitement. I just wanted to tell the world I had made it. It was as though someone had given me permission to be totally absorbed in my wedding - the very thing that Ron, my daughters, in fact everyone had used to keep me going and something I had aimed for, so I embarked on phone call after phone call sharing with everyone who would listen about my excitement.

How fantastic my dress was, it was perfect and amazing, everything could be covered up, tucked in and pushed up and 'what every women needs' - the most amazing invention ever had just put the icing on the cake! So everyone needed to be told.

During a last minute visit by my daughter Kelly (a now very heavily pregnant Kelly) and several bridesmaids dress fittings later, I was embarking on a usual 'tell the world' telephone relay – raving on about my perfect dress, chicken fillets etc, etc.

Kelly was sat beside me laughing hysterically every time I raved on about my chicken fillets! So were my friends! Everyone was so excited for me and I thought that my lovely story of chicken fillets was too much for them to contain!

After my final phone call I was left feeling so happy but then, within minutes my glee turned to embarrassment and shock!

You see, as I had looked at Kelly, who appeared as though she was about to give birth, holding on to baby bump with an almost look of desperation, legs crossed and tears of laughter dripping from her cheeks, it suddenly dawned on me that she wasn't laughing with me – but at me!

I frowned and waited impatiently as she tried to find breath to point out a mistake in my description of the "little miracles" that had given my figure such definition.

It came to light that my amazement about the miracle of "chicken fillets" had now been described, in my excitement, as "chicken drumsticks!"

But I had not made this mistake with just one phone call! Oh no! When Susan makes a mistake it has to be much bigger than just once! With every call I had raved on about the wonder of "chicken drumsticks!" and how wonderful they made me look!

Quite how fillets became drumsticks I was at a loss to understand or remember, but it didn't matter really - it was just typical of me! A normal Susan mistake with words! How wonderful - normality!

My fairy-tale wedding day was nearly here.

Doubting Thomas

As I lay in bed waiting for my tiredness to fade into a rested sleep, the darkness of the night time didn't seem as final or unfriendly as the last time I spent gazing through the small gap in my bedroom curtains waiting for tomorrow to arrive. Although my battle felt like a life time away my thoughts drifted back to my times of despair, fear and how I didn't know whether I had enough faith to believe I would get through the battle, let alone whether I could hang onto my belief in God. Staring at the gap in my curtains I realised that my life from tomorrow was about to change again.

Over the last few months I had been totally reliant on people and had to trust everyone - the hospital, Ron, family, friends and even God and although I realise I didn't have a choice in the matter, I was now faced with the realism that I had made the choice in marrying Ron, and for a few moments if I'm really honest, I had a real moment of panic. What was I doing?

As daft as it sounds I hadn't really thought about the fact that my long term commitment to Ron should have included trusting him, although he never gave me cause not to. However, I had vowed never to really trust anyone let alone a man ever again, and to be truthful it didn't really matter to me that I had this view, I had just accepted that this was how I was and it was normal for me. Now any sensible woman would have thought this through before saying the big YES, but as I have said trust didn't seem to matter - I could manage without it, until now when it felt as though it seemed to matter.

Now I know it may sound strange and mixed up, after all if anyone had deserved to earn my trust Ron did, especially after what he had been through over the last few months. But now I was faced with the fact that tomorrow I was embarking on a commitment to trust someone - Ron, when I had the choice to trust and not when this choice was taken away from me. But could I do it or even dare to do it?

All kinds of thoughts ran through my mind. All the rubbish that your head gets full of when you panic, from the betrayal of trust from my thirty year relationship, the impact of it on my lack of trust of my family, friends and my father.

As if that wasn't enough, what about God?

Could I, would I, do I want to ever be able to truly trust Him when you could say I had the choice? Did I have enough room in my heart to allow this word that had a life changing meaning to grow into a secure anchor? My mind felt as though it started to speak even more clearly, and my inner discussions began to ask more searching questions - all of which felt as though they were wrapped in a blanket of doubt.

What about God? Is he real? Or was it all fear?

Was it the fear that made me believe God was with me? How could I be sure I wasn't just imagining everything that had happened to me?

As I recall this moment while writing, I have to admit again I felt rather shallow and embarrassed. After everything I had been through, so many ways in which God had been with me, even making his presence and love so real - yet still I had doubt in the quiet times and allowed all the fears and lack of trust to cause me to panic.

I'm not saying that it's not right to question, after all I was making a commitment to Ron and I suppose trusting God in some respect with my future and I know everyone can have a moment, but why, after everything, was I still questioning if there was a God? I had personally had the experiences lived the experiences, yet here I was questioning them.

I found myself making an 'off the cuff' comment under my breath as I lay in the quiet of the night - 'talk about a doubting Thomas'. I wasn't looking for anything from the bible or even looking for inspiration, but a comment can have so much meaning – even an off the cuff one.

The bible talks about Thomas who was one of the twelve disciples.

Thomas had spent so much time with Jesus, but yet had still doubted when others told him that they had seen him after he had been crucified. So even the people closest to Jesus can have their doubts and I guess that doubts on their own are not so bad, especially if they cause you to ask the right questions, which God can then answer.

No sooner had I talked through my doubts both of Ron and God, one by one I began to be gently reminded about the different things that had happened to me over the last few months, in short, comforting glimpses of how in my times of need I was never let down by God, or Ron. He even gave Ron, my family and my friends the strength to cope and believe when I had no strength to.

I found the feeling of assurance and peace that had risen from my heart into my mind, enabled me to feel that tomorrow was the start of a journey which was going to lead to a greater level of trust with every step I took.

I didn't for one minute think that I would be lying in my bed the night before I was getting married, catching glimpses of my life and battle over the last few months and feeling a sense of victory and peace, but also an excitement about my new life ahead.

'We made it'

The morning of our wedding had arrived.

We had decided during one of our dreaming moments, when Ron was trying to help me be brave, that on the morning of our wedding we would call into town for our breakfast at a little café! You know - the type of café where you walk into a mist of thick heavy smog of bacon and sausage aroma, and it brings an amazing feeling of comfort (if you like that sort of thing, that is!)

For me the bacon, mushrooms and tomato juice was a feast, and one of my favourite foods and I even managed to eat a little of it, so that day, it felt like a meal fit for a queen.

Driving down into town we were like two children sneaking out of the house and up to mischief, we had such a laugh. After our amazing breakfast we parted company and our well thought out plans began to fall into place.

Before too long I was sitting, my hair neatly in place and Paula lovingly 'putting my face on' for me, then without warning my home in its quiet and calm state, changed into a flurry of activity, fun, and laughter. Children, mums, dresses, tights, curling tongs, lippy, friends and the photographer, just seemed to appear from nowhere.

We had agreed that we would make our wedding an experience for everyone, so we had an army of bridesmaids and page boys and had arranged for the children to get dressed in their wedding attire at the bungalow. Then as a treat everyone was to travel to the wedding in two stretch limos. As for me, the plan was for my mother and brother-in-law Peter, who had agreed to step in for Steve to give me away, to travel with me in a fabulous big cream and black chariot.

During the morning, for a brief moment, I found that time once again stood still and as I was sitting prepared for my moment to arrive, I gazed at the sun filled scene in my lounge that was before me. So much excitement, love and fun were being displayed. As I watched I mentally took a picture of it all, and as the sun was releasing its rays of love and life into the room, I felt it signalled the beginning of the dream that I had only hoped for.

I didn't want to miss out on any of the excitement of the children, so in my partly prepared wedding dress I eagerly escorted everyone outside to the cars. I think at this point I found myself as excited and as giddy; as them, their faces were such a picture of wonder and life, which was worth every moment of panic.

After waving everyone off, and walking back into the quiet bungalow, the stillness was such a contrast. The calmness had returned to my home and I was for a few moments all alone.

I must admit I had a few tears well up from within. I thought of my father and felt the disappointment and hurt that he was not here to see me today. I thought of Steve, and felt sad that he did not make it; I knew he would have been so proud. But then it was time to go, Peter was there at my side, and his reassuring hug stole my sad moment away.

Before many minutes it was my turn to walk to my beautiful chariot waiting for me. To my surprise many of my neighbours came out to see me off and an even more wonderful surprise, Lucy one of my ladies in blue, stood waiting to see me. As she made a last minute adjustment to my wedding lace coat for me to ensure I was perfect I left, waving to everyone. I was so touched to see them there, even the old guys on the street; what a surprise.

As I sat in the back of the wedding car with my mother, listening to Peter chatting away to the driver, I looked at the beautiful countryside and the scene playing before me. I had played this scene so many times in my imagination, especially during difficult and scary moments over the last few months, hardly daring to believe this day would arrive. But now it was happening, the day had started and I was on my way to my dream.

There was almost a surreal atmosphere in the car.

My mother sat beside me and I felt her sense of loss without Steve, and she, I knew, felt my excitement at my moment. Neither of us wanted to steal from each other the enormity of what we were both feeling, and yet, the contrast of our feelings was evident to us both – creating an awkwardness neither of us wanted to highlight. So we just chatted politely to each other, much like strangers do, when they share a brief moment – and actually, until very recently, that is exactly what my mother and I had been for many years – strangers. I knew many bridges had been built and I was so pleased she was here with me, and I knew that she wanted to be here, but still…sometimes polite chat is all you can do to get through.

Driving down the small windy road on the Thoresby estate, we seemed to slowly crawl towards the edge of the wall to reveal the beautiful fairy tale building lit up by the wonderful sun revealing all its splendour. This building was the typical 'princess' castle - the type fairy tales are made of - and one I had been dreaming of for months.

As we drove towards the clock tower, the months of living with the cancer, the fears, despair and disappointments were firmly placed in my memories, and once again I was walking into a clock tower door towards my future, only this time it was with the man that helped love me back to life and had become my life and my dream. This time it was clearly different from my younger years - and the peace, love and hope for my future was now waiting behind the large wooden doors.

This beautiful building - with its stately and elegant staircase and wonderful great hall - looked as though it had been transported from a special time in history where beauty and elegance was tastefully created in the oak panels! Everything was perfect and the romance was sealed with a grand piano playing softly in the background.

Ron and I had sat in the great hall many times in the past; just dreaming and trying to imagine the emotions and excitement we would feel when we made it to our special day.

Today was that special day and as I slowly walked up the staircase to the grand hall, with all the children with me, I truly felt like the Cinderella of the ball.

Standing in the library with Peter, the bridesmaids and the page boys waiting for their cue to enter into the wedding room, I was amazed that everything had gone to plan. All the children had behaved themselves and they had been so perfect - it was as though they knew how important this day had become to me!

And as one by one they disappeared into the room, Peter and I were left for what seemed such a long time.

Listening to the music from the wedding room, the library appeared to change from a large austere dusty room which smelt of history, into a warm and friendly one waiting to release a special moment and give birth to a new life.

When we began to hear the classical song I had chosen begin to build to the point I was to walk into my new life, Peter and I slowly started to make our way through the large oak carved doors.

The Blue Settee

Now this should have been the most romantic moment ever, and one I have to say I had played in my mind many times while listening to this music, especially when I was trying to be positive on a bad day.

But as Peter and I walked into the back of the room behind a podium full of flowers which hid my immediate entrance - (which also tantalised everyone and made a fabulous entrance for me) I let out a gasp and giggled uncontrollably. You see when Ron and I had visited the wedding co-ordinator, several times we had discussed the music I had chosen, but the problem was that the music could not be played on the normal music system of the hall as this fed into all the rooms open to the public, so they had a small CD player for the room. Now if you could have seen the size of this 'thing' – well, let me just say, I have one similar on my kitchen side and this 'thing' just didn't work for me. The room Ron and I had chosen for our wedding venue – the 'Blue' room was so beautiful with large bay windows, fire places and very very high walls with blue silk wallpaper that seem to reach for the sky before hitting the ornate ceiling. Although I had voiced my concern regarding this music 'thing' to the co-ordinator I had accepted that it would be okay on the day and my favourite music would be heard.

Now what I was seeing, as Peter and I walked into the room was my wedding co-ordinator at the back of the room balancing two three foot speakers with the biggest smile on her face. No wonder my music sounded amazing blasting out. I later found out that she had borrowed them and wanted everything perfect for me as she too had been party to my struggles to get to this day. This was a lovely gesture and the little things that she and her staff did throughout the afternoon to ensure everything was perfect was a beautiful gift.

As Peter and I turned the corner into the room my giggling was interrupted by an amazing scene. As I recall this special moment it still brings tears to my eyes. You see I was met with a wonderful room full of sunshine, everything seem to sparkle like a diamond catching the light with so many beautiful colours dancing off the walls and ceilings, and a sea of never-ending love, smiles and tears that embraced me with every step I took.

As Peter and I walked towards the front of the room I felt as though I was gliding gracefully towards my future. I knew this was the right thing for me and God was with me. I was taken back by seeing so many faces smiling; as I looked I couldn't help but notice how everyone looked so lovely, everyone had made such an effort and invested into my day. I can remember seeing most people and taking a mental picture as I slowly made my way towards Ron, but I remember very clearly catching Janette my boss's eye and my smiles conveying to her 'yes I made it Janette'!

As I got nearer to the front I saw my youngest sisters Penny and Avril, both full of smiles and tears - they were so brave for me and they must have been hurting so. As I drew nearer to the front of the room I saw that Ron was waiting for me. I can honestly say that I have never been as sure of anything as I was then. He had willed me better and cared for me so much and now he was waiting for me to call me his wife and I had made it.

It was a lovely simple ceremony, but it meant so much and we have a fabulous photograph which shows the utter joy in our faces as the registrar said the words 'I pronounce you husband and wife'. The picture captures the moment I said 'we made it' - that simple statement was loaded with so much meaning. We had made it! I had made it! The very thing I had hung onto through my darkest days - I had made it! I had left the cancer behind, I had beaten it. I had seen and experienced God clearly in my life through this illness and it had brought me into a place I had never experienced before. He gave me a new life, a new life with a depth of love in it I had never had before. It was truly an amazing wedding.

Ron was not a 'church goer' although he believed in God, but he had agreed that having a Blessing after the wedding ceremony was the perfect start to our life together and one that would cement and acknowledge that He was part of our marriage and future life together. The perfect person to perform this for us was my daughter Kelly's husband Adrian. So with tongue in cheek I was now sitting waiting for him to say a little something about me.

I have to confess I was a little apprehensive as he started the introduction to the Blessing with his views on his mother-in-law, me. As I look back on this I had every right to be apprehensive as I can honestly say that I had been more than the typical mother-in-law we often hear about in the jokes of many a famous comedian. The 'dragon' or 'tyrant' would have properly described me. Adrian, a very gracious man, was very nice and to my relief said some funny and very kind things about his mother-in-law.

Having him and Mark, the leader of my church, pray for us as husband and wife, completed a very special wedding and left my heart smiling.

While they and everyone else was praying, I remember thinking that this was a very special moment and that all three men represented the different people in my life this day. Mark represented my church family who from that first prayer in his and Carolyn's home had stood with me before God, trusting in Him to bring me through. Back then I had entered into that prayer time with very little faith to believe myself, but so touched that they would care enough to believe for me. Back then I had not dared to hope for my healing, let alone hope that one I would be standing here today.

Adrian represented not only my children and family, and their hopes and beliefs for me, but he represented his church in the Midlands, and the way they had taken me into their hearts and embraced hope and faith in God for me. And Ron, standing there, represented my friends who, although claimed no faith in God for themselves, were prepared to embrace my faith and to join in this prayer that Mark and Adrian were raising up for Ron and I.

A prayer of thanksgiving for our lives, a prayer of hope for our future, and a prayer of joy that this day was here and we could all celebrate together. Just a truly perfect day!

"We made it"

My New Life

"One pina colada Mrs Barnett."

As I forced my eyes open, a large glass was placed under my chin by a very polite waiter who felt it necessary to give me a momentary break from the sun, whilst almost piercing the end of my nose and attaching a very large cherry on it. He obviously didn't think it was enough that I was glowing with the sun, but felt the need to want to make me look like Rudolph.

Trying to sit up gracefully was proving to be an impossible task. The waiter, who appeared to have the expertise and knowledge, took on a helping role by carefully placing my pina colada under my nose in order for me to follow its gliding path, giving me a sense of direction to the upright position. Undertaking this manoeuvre in a semi-conscious state was proving difficult. This required me to stretch my right arm out to the side to find my glasses, whilst placing my left arm over my bikini top just in case something was revealed that would shatter any momentary vision of elegance. This manoeuvre was later described by Ron as looking like a loud squawking duck undertaking an horizontal can-can while trying to desperately release its 'butt' from the frozen lake to take flight and was very far from graceful.

After successfully undertaking this task, trying to redeem any possible shred of elegance and demur, in addition to secretly scanning my neighbouring sun gods and goddesses, I was shocked by Ron's fits of laughter which seemed to signal to everyone around me to enter into the scene that was before them. As I was desperately trying to fathom out what was so funny, I discovered that I had not only put on Ron's glasses, which meant I was almost blind, but I was sitting trying to appear 'normal' with the yellow froth of the pina colada on the end of my nose and a red sticky trail from my chin down onto my chest finally showing a sun kissed cherry blob nestled nicely into the eggcup size crevice of my bikini.

My helpful, and ready for any eventuality, waiter presented Ron with a white napkin simply stating that this was for his wife's 'little predicament.'

After the slight distraction of my little mishap I soon settled down into the relaxing world of my honeymoon and before too long I was looking out to sea as we were sailing to our final destination on our Caribbean cruise. Everything looked so beautiful and blue; there didn't seem to be a distinction between the blue sea and the blue sky - everything appeared so perfect. You know when you look around and you get lost in a moment without consciously making the effort to do it, you just find yourself there? Well that's was I was doing - looking and being lost in the beauty of what was before me.

Seven months had passed since the day my new life as Mrs Barnett had started, and sixteen months after hearing the words 'sorry' and 'cancer' while sitting on the blue settee. That day seemed so far away; so many things had happened, some good, some bad, and some, well, *amazing*. And now I was sitting on a ship in the middle of the Caribbean ocean glancing into a few of the memories.

As I gazed at the graceful white waves as they slowly melted away into the bright blue picture before me, I never for one moment thought that one day I would be looking back at my life and seeing that it was so different. It felt so good.

You could say this feeling was because I was a fairly newly married woman and as the saying goes 'all loved up' and everything felt new. But as with most things in life you really don't know what you are missing in your life until something changes.

I now realise that what I thought was living pre my cancer battle, was truly not living. Although I had thought I had everything and was fairly content, I hadn't known what was missing until now.

So what was it that was missing? Well trying to find the word or words to describe a feeling that is as real and alive as I feel today has been very hard and has caused me to reflect on not only my journey, but on who I am and the experiences I have had throughout my life from childhood, upwards, until today. And how these experiences good or bad have moulded me into the woman I became 'warts and all'.

After doing this, I knew that throughout my life and the many difficulties I had faced both as a child and as an adult, all had resulted in my life being controlled by fear! So, therefore, I now knew that the missing ingredient in my life for all those years had been Peace.

Today I have a Peace which is real and indescribable. Although to be honest I still can worry and get upset, and this in itself could be argued as a contradiction, but what I mean is that I have a Peace and assurance that whatever I go through I know that God will be with me. Not because I have been told or I've become all religious, or it makes good reading but, because God showed himself to me throughout my journey. Even when I doubted He revealed himself or spoke to me. He never left me.

That has given me a Peace and assurance that whatever I face I know I will never ever be alone. Although I have said this many times throughout my Christian life and I felt I knew this to be true, because of this journey I have a clearer picture of how He *showed* me that He was with me, by my side giving me the strength to carry on. I now have a new understanding of this and what God can do. This has given me an amazing Peace and a love I had never ever truly felt or experienced.

While smiling at my thoughts of this amazing feeling, I continued to gaze at the path of the ship as it carved its way through the water. I noticed that the path was not straight, but at times showed sweeping and graceful lines with the white graceful waves dissolving into the blue picture. With every curve of the path it seemed to reflect the different directions that my own path in life had taken me. As the waves were outlining the path left behind, I associated this scene with my journey and although the ship continued carving its way to its destination, it was not only leaving behind a journey but continuing with a new one.

As I continued to enjoy the beautiful scene, I remembered how God had first revealed himself to me in a way that could not be dismissed as mere coincidence, or 'conjured up' or manipulated - you know the type of things people say when you tell them about God. I had even been heard to say the very same thing myself for many years when arguing with my mother and father-in-law as they attended church. In a dismissive way I would say, "It's all in your mind, it's all coincidence!" when they tried to tell me about their experiences. But then, it was my turn to have an experience that could not be described as a coincidence.

Shortly after I had started to come to church, I had been invited to a ladies convention. I had agreed to attend, not because I really wanted to after all who wants to spend an afternoon with a bunch of women at some women's thing knitting and doing craft things? (You know the view about the lady 'do-gooders' with blue rinses, smelling of lavender, nice flat sensible shoes, twin sets and pearls - as I thought.)

How wrong was I?

I didn't see one blue rinse although I probably saw a couple of sets of pearls. Well, this was my first experience with God. He revealed himself in such a way that it could not be a coincidence and evidently this was clearly what I had needed at the time. This experience had a profound effect on me.

Shortly after starting to come to church I said the prayer for God to enter into my life, to be part of my life and to learn to walk with Him. I remember the discussion I had with my spiritual mum and dad the pastor and his wife, (Mike and Yvonne) about this! Well, I say "discussion", but more often than not it was a slightly more heated one on my side than theirs I have to say, and one of many before making the final decision.

At the start my personal journey with Him all I wanted from Him was to show me He was real. I said that if He did this, then my commitment would be a 'proper' commitment - this is a perfect example of me being in control!

However, in the course of one of the many 'discussions' I remember thinking to myself that short of God tapping me on my forehead and saying that he was real and existed, I didn't think that I would ever really be convinced of this. But everyone was so lovely so it made a change and it was nice to be involved with something. So without realising I had set God a challenge.

Well the ladies convention was not what I was expecting and no, it wasn't knitting and crafts. I saw a lot of women of all ages young and old worshipping with such a passion, I was mesmerised by it. To be honest I couldn't understand why they were like it. I enjoyed the songs, but I was puzzled what was it that they had?

At the end of the 'preach', the pastor had asked if anyone would like to receive prayer. Not wanting to be the only one left out of our group, I thought I would give it a go. So I stood patiently not sure why, or what for. Then it was soon became my turn.

I had noticed that the women were closing their eyes; however, I had already made up my mind that my eyes were firmly staying open!

Out of respect for the man who was working so hard for God, I was prepared to bow my head slightly. After making a polite smile towards the nice man, I lowered my head - gazing at his shoes. After a few moments into what sounded like a very nice prayer which I have to say did alleviate some of my anxieties, he asked me to look at him. When I raised my head and nervously smiled at him he placed his finger onto the middle of my forehead gently tapping it. He then said that it was okay to ask questions but to ask them in love, for He was my God and He loved me - his child. With that the man smiled at me and walked way.

Shocked was an understatement! I had never said this to anyone, but this man knew what to say to me. God knew and He revealed Himself to me in a way that could not be a coincidence. Needless to say the songs that I sung after that event meant something different to me, the difference being - I believed that God was real. He had shown me, He had given me a new life and a life with hope.

And now fifteen years later He had again shown me that He was still in my life. He was still my loving Father, and He was still my God. But with all the hurts and disappointments, lack of trust and fear that I had been experiencing, God made his presence known to me in an unquestionable and dramatic way. He knew what it would take; He knew what I needed.

Gladys

Another day of sunshine and another time of reflection. Although I have realised whilst writing my story that I appear to have done a lot of that, I guess we always do it and quite often without making a conscious effort. So there I was again, undertaking a slow walk round the ship, taking in the warmth of the sun and lovely scene around me and feeling contented and relaxed.

My thoughts again wandered into my journey.

When I had said the words 'I do' on the day that Ron and I had stood with all our friends and family in a united moment of victory, the day that we had all been waiting for and working towards, I had thought that that would be where my story would finish, that that was the end of the battle and the place of victory and peace.

However, as I have shared with you, I feel that although God had brought me to the place of Peace and into a new journey of learning to trust it also seemed that God had more lessons to show me through the journey after the wedding.

This time my thoughts were unexpectedly about my ex mother-in-law, Gladys, and how she lost her own battle shortly after my wedding.

When I started to put my thoughts and feelings into written words to share my story many months ago, I knew that Gladys was to be included in my reflection of my journey and although I didn't know why, I tried many times to think it through, and I had even tried to guess why. All I knew was that my desire to include her was very real. However, when I started to write her name it then became very clear.

I had known Gladys since I was fourteen and until I started my treatment we had regularly remained in touch. Gladys had for many years, since being a young woman, suffered with acute rheumatoid arthritis and now in her eighties she was facing the loss of a leg and losing battle with the disease that had crippled her for most of her adult life. Throughout my battle with cancer Maxine had kept me up to date as to how she was doing in hospital.

Unfortunately I had been advised that I could not visit her due to my treatment and susceptibility to infections, but Maxine and I had 'sneaked' in to visit her after my big day. It had been lovely to see her, even though she was visibly undertaking her own battle, she still managed to eat some wedding cake.

As we were leaving I turned round and waved to her and as she waved back it felt really good to see her. I didn't see her as my ex mother-in-law but just a lady I knew really well who had fought long and hard with a constant unrelenting battle with pain for most of the time I had known her.

However, I knew when looking back at her that there was also something different. It wasn't that I felt sorry for her, or I even recognised that she was more ill than perhaps we really knew, but as we smiled at each other I knew what it was. At that moment I had been able to connect with her in a way I had never felt I had done before.

I didn't see a very poorly lady, I saw a very strong and courageous woman with a determined and often stubborn character which for years had meant that she did not give in to her illness and hung onto life and lived it. I hadn't seen that before.

Gladys left us all for the place she longed to be in her darkest days on the 2nd June.

Gladys, just like Steve had been, was a significant loss in my children's life. As for me, she had been part of my own childhood and teenage years as well as a large part of my adult life with all its good and bad times. I had worked through the loss of Steve and faced my own mortality, now I was to face the loss of Gladys and my past life so very quickly after losing Steve. As I started to write about Gladys, it didn't cause me to look at my mortality but to look at her life and what that life had meant to me.

I earlier described my relationship with my son-in- law as the typical mother-in-law, the 'dragon' or 'the tyrant'. If I'm honest I would probably also describe myself as the dreaded daughter-in-law and I know that I was more than a handful throughout my years of being part of Gladys' life, and would often have given her many headaches and probably lots of heartache. I know I wasn't always the easiest person to get on with and I'm sure she would say the same thing herself, but she was the perfect sparring partner!

When Maxine brought messages of encouragement from Gladys during my treatment, I found it a very humbling experience. However, I also felt guilty. You see through the years, I found it fairly easy to accept that Gladys was in constant pain and although I knew that her illness was hard for her to cope with at times, my acceptance of her situation, if I was truthful, was probably more often in a matter of fact way and probably not always in the most caring way. It wasn't that I didn't care, because I did, but we can become desensitised to people's suffering without realising it.

I'm sure I wasn't on my own, and realistically I am not sure that we can really fully understand unless we have been or are going through it ourselves. And even then everyone's story is very different. We become so busy with lives, children and jobs, all of which are genuine, but in all our business and fast living we sometimes forget to show how much we care and give time to care.

I realise now, as I look back at the years of knowing Gladys, I didn't have an understanding of what living with pain was really like or how it can affect you in so many ways. Not just physically but emotionally and how your life can so easily become the illness and pain you live with. This way of living can leave very little space for anything else at times, except breathing.

So what about Gladys?

Well, through the years I had seen her cry many times when she was in so much pain, but the truth is that I had also seen her praise God while in pain. I had seen her unable to stand to her feet due to her pain, but have seen her stand firm in her belief in God's healing and speak about her understanding of His amazing truth. I have seen her struggle to walk into church but able to walk to the front of the church to declare God's love and encourage others.

I'm not saying for one moment she was perfect and I don't want you to think that I am trying to describe a saint, because she wasn't, although she was often more saint like than me. But the fact is, until I had my own journey, I didn't know or understand what and how Gladys' faith was the foundation of her life. How her belief and trust in God sustained her so many times but also gave her hope and strength to carry on when her pain was unbearable.

I had been living with my pain, treatment, the roller-coaster rides of emotions and fears for only a short time, yet here was a woman who had been part of my life for so many years and fought this battle on a daily basis, and I can only now appreciate how important her faith was and what a difference it made to her.

Now, and only now, do I understand how important it was to have a strong foundation in God. How important it is to believe and trust in God and how this can give you the strength and hope to carry on, for me that was all I had and therefore it was all I could do during my darkest days.

When I look back at Gladys' life, I think that I am only now beginning to know the real woman behind the pain and suffering that I had associated with her. Now I can see the real Gladys - a Godly woman with determination and strength of character and a belief in God I never understood before.

Gladys not only had support from her family but also had support from a small group of friends whose commitment to her through the years was evident and unwavering. I knew this support was important to her on a weekly basis and I knew that the prayer support from the church was a vital link for Gladys. What I didn't understand was what a difference support and prayers make when times are tough and hanging onto life is hard.

For me the many cards and messages received throughout the weeks and months of my treatment meant so much to me. They felt like a vital link to the outside world which showed that it still had a place for me. I recall a couple of times when things were really tough; receiving messages from people I knew when I had been the youth leader within the church, who were now grown up with their own families; and churches sending messages of love, support and prayers, which was so encouraging and comforting. I was aware that there were so many prayers being lifted up for me, from people who knew me, and from people who I had never met but cared enough to believe in healing for me.

The kindness of people outside of the church was also a blessing, from past and new friends, colleagues and friends through work, receiving many gifts, and cards throughout my illness and treatment was overwhelming.

Even when writing about this I feel very emotional. You see I never, for one moment, realised in my busy life that this kind of support was vital. People really need to know you and others care. I now appreciate and understand the importance of being aware that people are offering prayer support and how this kind of support can help when you're in a raging battle, whatever that battle may be. I now personally know it does make a difference, even if you yourself don't fully believe or trust.

Gladys knew what it was to have people that were faithful in standing beside her through the years with her battle with pain, and again until my experience I didn't understand what a difference it makes having people standing with you in your battle and this is something I won't ever forget. Showing someone you care – makes a difference, standing with someone makes a difference, believing for someone gives Hope.

The Pouch

Another day of sunshine, and feeling so good to be alive! The sea looked different today; the colour and depth of it appeared to have changed, which meant while looking out at the path we had left behind, the milky emerald blue trail looked more prominent against the ink blue rippling blanket.

I remembered how Gladys' funeral had been such a 'bitter free' day considering how much of my past was there that day, and how different it could have been had I not gone through what I had in the past months.

Facing my ex-husband and his new partner at the funeral would probably have once upon a time devastated me, or at least caused me to feel anger and resentment, but with the new hope and fresh outlook that God had given me, I had been able to attend the funeral with my new found peace and I had been amazed at how little I had felt towards the man who had reeked so much devastation in my life. I had been able to say goodbye to Gladys one last time, and in a sense really say goodbye, once and for all, to my past and had let it all go, the good and the bad.

I began to think how life started to get back into a routine after Gladys' funeral.

Before too long things began to change physically, in terms of the effects left on me by the treatment and I didn't seem able to cope with the changes with my mouth. I don't know whether I had been a little unrealistic, naive, because I just didn't even stop to think that my lifestyle would be affected or would change as a result of my battle.

However, all the elation and relief I had experienced when they informed me that the tumour had in fact gone had soon been forgotten, and if I'm honest I began to be a little resentful. I wasn't going down the path of "why me?" but I was finding it difficult to adjust to my new way of living and, as I'm sure you may have gathered while reading about my journey, I'm not very gracious at times.

Some people may perhaps feel that once again I was being ungrateful, after all I was alive, my life had turned around; I had come through a battle with an outcome that was not expected – the most that had been hoped for was that the tumour would shrink enough to remove surgically, but now I had been informed it had gone completely.

So why was I having difficulty with adjusting to the after effects of the treatment? Shouldn't I be grateful? Shouldn't I be able to take it all in my stride? After all, it wasn't as bad as going through the treatment with all its struggles and pain, was it?

But the reality was, I knew all this and I wanted to be strong enough and determined to accept the changes, take it all in my stride, get on with life, but I just couldn't do it. I couldn't accept and adjust to the changes and not because I didn't want to. I felt I just couldn't climb over the wall of resentment, confusion and horror to get to the place of acceptance of change. The wall was too high.

But as I sat and watched the ship continue on its journey leaving behind the path moving slowly away further from the horizon, I recalled having this very conversation with Angela, my Macmillan nurse, shortly after my treatment ended.

I hadn't been expecting to see her that day. She had been in the area and thought she would pop in, which was lovely given that her role in my treatment and life was supposed to have been done with. I was so relieved to see her, especially as I had got myself all upset.

Angela sat and allowed me the space to pour out my heart and as usual I did it well and to my embarrassment. You would have been forgiven for thinking, if you had been sat in the room, that once again my whole world had come tumbling down around me.

My lack of saliva still meant eating was a problem without drinking gallons of water. Getting through the night without having to wake up and sip water with the inevitable ten mile trek to the loo was also causing a lot of problems. Although walking with my eyes closed and finding the toilet was an achievement I was getting proud of.

The lack of taste and how this affected what I ate - everything still had very little or no taste, therefore eating was difficult and not enjoyable at all. Many things I couldn't eat either because of the consistency which meant I couldn't swallow them, or the feeling of having a thick "gung" in my mouth, making it impossible to digest.

The constant focus and battle with my mouth and with food, and trying to prevent the ongoing infections let alone the swelling around my jaw line, was a lifestyle I never imagined would be mine. I felt that it just wasn't fair, hadn't I won my battle? But this didn't feel like a victory. It felt like the war was still on.

Oh yes, I forgot about the pouch under my chin.

This was just the icing on the cake! Not only had I had to put up with the crevices, and the remnants from a crow's disco on my face, now I had my 'wonderful' pouch to add to the character of my portrait. Every time I looked into the mirror all I saw was a reflection that resembled a lizard; you know the one that has the big pouch? Well that's the one! (Although when I've looked at photos' it wasn't as bad, and I wish no disrespect to anyone who has a bit of a pouch, but as usual I had blown everything out of all proportion and a drama was unfolding.)

One day looking in the mirror, I even found myself saying 'you're not a very good Christian you can't even accept your pouch!"

I don't for one minute think I am describing a godly woman, with an assurance in herself that comes from knowing a God of love and acceptance. But that's how it was, and nevertheless I continued with this behaviour for a while.

And it got worse! This pouch was my problem! And the word cancer had faded into the horizon of my past. I found that I was beginning to balance my head on the back of one of my hands in a bid to hide my pouch or flatten it. You know the way you would if you were posing for a facial portrait. I convinced myself I looked graceful or that no one would notice that my hand was stuck under my chin. In truth I probably looked awkward and strange especially when I also found myself walking around with my hand stuck onto my pouch without realising it, which must have attracted more attention than my pouch.

Having taken Angela through my one thousand and one problems, it became pretty clear to her that now my life felt as though it was just my mouth, food, swelling and my pouch. Would there be no end to it all?

When I paused to take a breath, Angela smiled and once again offered reassurance that my difficulty in adjusting to change was part of a normal process. I was relieved to hear it, although I don't think she meant my 'graceful pose' was normal.

Shortly after Angela stated that she would speak to the consultant at the hospice where she was based, I was sitting in the reception area waiting nervously.

The Blue Settee

The consultants at the cancer hospital were fantastic and looked after me well. My local hospital continued with my care and also did it well , so having said all that, would this new consultant think that after all the hard work of the hospitals, I was just a problem patient, ungrateful, or a 'Moaning Minnie' or whatever you want to call it?

I couldn't have been so wrong! After my initial shock of "oh my word this young woman looks like she should still be in school!" I took her through all my difficulties, my worries around coping or not, as the case may be. Her reassuring nods in the right places meant that my anxiety was controlled enough to tell her it all.

The only thing I was too embarrassed to tell her about, was my pouch or to be exact the problem I feel about my pouch.

As she began to talk to me, slowly working through each of my symptoms one by one, I started to have a different understanding of the reasons why these individual symptoms were happening. As someone once said, "knowledge is power!"

With each explanation and suggestion that she made, the wall of resentment, confusion and horror began to be taken down, brick by brick, and the gateway to acceptance and peace appeared for me to walk through.

However, I must tell you about the greatest revelation! a tip that had been given to her by other patients when their mouths had become sticky and creamy with thick fermented saliva.

208

She told me about the cleansing effect of drinking a bit of lager and for a brief moment I smiled to myself 'Wow! Normality!'

I had tried a little bit of alcohol a few times but it either tasted terrible, or it caused discomfort. Not that I needed to drink, but it is nice to socialise a little and feel normal. This meant that not only would I be able to enjoy half a pint with friends and family but I could also count it as medicinal!!

Just as we were finishing our discussion around the different instructions for my prescription support, and feeling relieved at what an amazing difference it makes understanding things, she announced the final thing she needed to do was examine under my chin.

In all the excitement about the revelations around my symptoms and possible strategies for dealing with them, I had totally forgotten about my pouch, but I think part of it was that I was too embarrassed to bring it up.

Although, whichever way I look at it, it just comes down to my vanity, doesn't it? And, as you have already read, I had already had a few "moments" like this throughout my journey you would have thought that I should have learned!

But I didn't and so now this was my latest vanity drama.

I tried to pass it off as not a problem, but I think she knew it was; after all it appeared that I had a problem with everything else!

The Blue Settee

When she started to examine me, she talked me through the reasons behind the pouch being there something about fluid and lymph glands and manually moving it. I couldn't believe what I was hearing; I was stuck for words, which was a first. I had been so fixated on my pouch and now, not only did I understand why it was there, but soon I was to meet a nurse who would show me how to manually move this fluid around to disperse it.

Halleluiah my pouch was to go!

I left the hospice feeling wonderful and fully armed to face the battle of coping with my mouth. I'm not sure how I got home; it must have been on a cloud because I remember nothing.

It's strange when you look back and reflect on situations that you have been in, how you sometimes can't believe what happened or how you handled a situation. For my part as I write about this time, I do feel embarrassed and a bit ashamed about how I had handled the issue not only with my mouth, but how I got into this fixated state over my pouch and my looks. However, sometimes situations slowly smother you and take over your mind and thoughts without realising it, and the problem or situation becomes your life, and you seem to sleep, breathe, and eat it all - with no room for anything or anyone else. It can be so hard to get off this path once you're on it.

I burst into the bungalow, shouting loudly for Ron. He appeared at the kitchen door with a slightly worried look on his face, not sure what was happening. I excitedly and hurriedly told him it all, even my pouch news. But this excited state was interrupted when I became aware that Ron was not really listening very closely.

I was a little bemused as to why Ron was not sharing in my excitement about my pouch. So I followed him into the kitchen repeating the garbled story in a bid to get him to see the fantastic news that my pouch was to go.

Ron calmly placed down the wooden spoon he was stirring the pan with, turned the gas ring off, flicked his tea towel over his shoulder (you know the 'man way' of handling the tea towel) and then turned to look at me and announced with a smile on his face, that he didn't know what all the fuss was about, after all God has a pouch.

I wasn't sure I heard right and I was slightly speechless!

When my puzzled look signalled to Ron to repeat his statement, he repeated, "I don't know why you are so worried about your pouch Susan, God has a pouch. So if God has a pouch and I love you with or without one, what's your problem?"

Well this wasn't the response I was looking for or even imagined. I couldn't even bring to mind what my problem was with my pouch other than just my vanity, but I also didn't understand what he meant. So while watching him lovingly prepare a plate of food for our dinner, I calmed down and talked him through what the consultant had said about my symptoms and the things I could do to help me cope with them. Then while sitting at the dinner table I rather sheepishly began once again to approach the subject of my pouch.

I could tell that Ron knew I was trying to bring it up and he wasn't making it easy for me - changing the subject, embarking on our usual banter - when in the end I could no longer hold onto my curiosity any more. Again, I asked him what he meant by that God has a pouch.

Ron smiled as he reminded me that when he came to church with me a few weeks ago, he heard the speaker say that we were made in the image of God, "So if you look like God then he must have a pouch!"

I was so shocked by this, all I could do was laugh and I laughed so much that tears were rolling down my face.

When my laughing calmed down to a giggle, Ron described how for weeks he had seen me get obsessed by my pouch, how I had walked around holding onto my head as if it was going to fall off my shoulders, going on about how my looks had changed, referring to my crows disco and crevices. He said that he knew that I had not been coping and that although he had tried to help, I had kept him and others at bay. He reminded me that we had been through such a lot and that we would work anything out together with or without a pouch on the scene.

Then he landed me with another gem.

He said, "What about God and your faith over the last few weeks Susan? You didn't want my help or comfort, so did you go to God for help? Wasn't he there for you through your battle?"

To be honest I can't recall my exact answer to this, but I know I was desperately trying to make excuses and reasons as to why I hadn't, and I felt uncomfortable by the question because I knew I hadn't gone to anyone.

As he was tidying the table in preparation to take the dinner plates away he said, "This is what I think Susan. I heard that story in church about the two sisters when Jesus came to the house to visit. The speaker talked about how one sister sat and listened to Jesus and how the other one was a bit like you, running around like a headless chicken doing everything else but spend time with Him."

Ron then went on to say "What do I know Susan? You're the Christian!', but then added; "I figure that, according to that story, you might have been better if you had spent a bit of time with God rather that getting obsessed with your pouch. At the least it would have given my ears a rest. Do you know you were doing my head in! So does this now mean that the real Susan is back - crow's feet and all?"

I never learn!

During my journey I have encountered many people and been in many situations that it is only now as I sit writing about them, that I realise the profound and lasting effect they have had on my world. Reflecting on my healing process I could not write this book without mentioning Christine, the lymphedema nurse whose care of me became a welcome refuge from the world of work, family and responsibility.

The Blue Settee

Her job was to gently stroke my body in the areas where the fluid had built up as a result of the lymph nodes not working. Radiotherapy causes the lymph nodes to stop working around the area where it is concentrated in my case, in my facial area. Therefore, fluid had to be moved manually and this was Christine's job to caress away the fluid gathering in certain areas around my face, neck and head. I can tell you, there was no nicer therapy than this! One of the perks of having cancer I guess!

I began to really look forward to our weekly encounters and I saw it as my final battle with the pouch, because this was the area that would benefit most from the treatment. In compliance with the treatment I was required to give myself a facial massage every day to disperse the fluid in my pouch, face neck and head, and you can rest assured that I carried out this duty with military precision, determined that the pouch was to go and I would do everything in my power to ensure that not one trace of the wretched thing would remain!

Meeting with Christine every week was not only a time of therapy where my physical needs were being taken care of, and to elicit further information regarding the care of my mouth, but also a place where I could share with this kind woman my story as it unfolded. I was beginning to write this book, and I would share my progress with her, and she would listen attentively and ask me about it all. I would talk about how God had been with me helping me, and how he was with me guiding me through the process of writing my story. She would stroke and I would speak, and it was a lovely time.

On my final visit with her we sat looking at my before and after photographs, taken to show the progress we had made with the treatment. I was stunned at the difference the treatment had made on my appearance; in fact I learned that the progress made had been so remarkable that Christine had been showing the photographs to her colleagues and other patients to encourage other sufferers that this treatment really works. It was nice to know that my recovery had been so evident and the before and after photographs would be used in this way.

Christine began to tell me that she was also a church goer, and that she and the young consultant that I had met at the hospice, and a few other nurses there had formed a prayer group, and at this prayer group Christine was encouraging them all with my story. This was when I realised that not only had my presence there been beneficial to me, but that my life, my story and my journey were also being used to affect others positively and to encourage them. This meant so much to me and it really confirmed to me why I needed to write this book.

There were people out there who needed to hear my story and be encouraged by it. There were people who needed to know that amongst all the hardships of life and cancer and death and illness, there was hope, there were miracles, there was joy and there was goodness. There were people who needed to be encouraged not to give up,

The Blue Settee

there were people who needed to know they were not alone, there were people who needed to know that ordinary men and women can stand together and find their way through life's battles by holding onto each other, holding onto faith and holding onto the knowledge that there is more to life than what we initially see with our eyes and hear with our ears.

The Titanic Experience

Standing at the front of the ship I felt like Rose and Jack in the film Titanic - before the sinking of course, full of hope and the future. For much of the cruise I had been sitting at the back of the ship thinking about the journey behind me, but now I was at the front of the ship looking forward, watching my future coming towards me. It was an exhilarating feeling and I can tell you that although my honeymoon cruise had been exciting, reflective and beautiful I was looking forward to going home, to my new life for real......

But of course, I knew now that this was not the start. I was already well on my way. I had been on my way since the day I picked up the pen to start writing this book. I had always known from that moment that this story was going to be interesting! I hadn't fully realised that looking back was going to take me to places that perhaps I had not expected to visit, but I also knew that this self-discovery, though at times uncomfortable, was not just about my healing, though of course it was all about that, it was also to offer some kind of healing to others.

I remember feeling like I was flying and as the future came towards me that I would embrace it full on with a new sense of peace and hope and assurance. I was standing there with my face up tilted towards the heavens, feeling the salty breeze and the warmth of the Caribbean sun on my skin and it was like being kissed by God the Father himself, a loving kiss that said it was all okay.

I had left my fears behind. There was no sense that any more healing needed to be done, that in the words of Jesus Christ "It is Finished!"

But as I embraced those words into my soul, little did I know that Jesus was smiling in amusement at me. In fact in the warmth of the sun and the coolness of the breeze, I may have been feeling the smile of God! Because in the words of the song "I ain't seen nothin' yet!"

Susan Barnett entered the Roy Todd Encounter Weekend Event a few months later, a woman with a smile on her face at the world. She had come to thank God for the healing that he had done in her life. She had come to stand on the stage, with familiar friends from the worship group, and to sing her praises to God. *This* Susan Barnett was the new me!!

A media clip depicting the journey of my life from the blue settee to this day was to be shown. This after all was a massive healing event, led by an Irish guy who had a gift of being able to talk about his faith in God as a healer and the person who can change your life. He had a "down to earth", "easy to understand" way of speaking, with touches of the Irish humour thrown in for good measure that really got people's attention.

I had been listening to Roy Todd since he was a young Evangelist starting out on his journey, and I was looking forward to hearing what he had to say and to seeing other people experience the healing hand of God. It was also a privilege to know that my story would be shared with the crowds in the church as a means of encouraging them to believe for great things!

Little did I know that God had a few more surprises in store for me!

The night was amazing and the media clip with me telling my story had a profound effect on not only me, as it was the first time I had heard it, but as I looked round the room I could see several people wiping tears from their faces.

I couldn't wait to see what God would do in terms of healing other people. Because he had healed me, I knew that he could, and would, heal others. And God did not fail to turn up that night. People were being healed all over the place and I was so happy for them. My heart was smiling and fit to burst.

The place was buzzing, and so was I.

When Roy did his appeal for people to go forward for healing, I had no thought of going forward. After all I was healed. My cancer was gone, the pouch was gone, and the job was accomplished.

Wasn't it?

But as I stood there watching people going forward to receive their healing, I suddenly felt an inexplicable prompting that I can't quite explain. There these people were, responding in faith and trust to God, the God that I knew quite well was capable of meeting their needs, and here was I standing, knowing full well that there was one area of my life that was still causing me problems – and I was not looking to God for the answer. What was wrong with me? After everything I had been through didn't I believe that God could meet this need?

You see, the problem was still the saliva issue. I have mentioned this before, but I think that because I had gotten so used to it, I had accepted that this was a part of my life I was going to just have to get used to.

It was the lack of saliva being produced in my mouth that was not only causing me sleepless nights and general discomfort when eating and talking, but was also the cause of monthly infections in my mouth. My mouth always felt sore and my tongue felt thick and swollen. But it was the lack of sleep that was the most distressing thing for me.

I still had to sip water before falling asleep, then having to sip water several times in the night and this of course would mean I was still undertaking nightly treks to the bathroom which was no longer funny, all of which was contributing to me having to exist on only a few minutes a time of sleep.

I would like to write that after realising this fact, I ran to the front of the church shouting hallelujah and declaring to all around me that God will heal me, because I knew that He could do it. But I didn't, and although I was a little slow off the starting line, I did make my way to the front of the church.

Through the years of being a Christian, I had seen and taken part in appeals for healing and if I'm honest, sometimes responding as I felt that this was expected -'it was the done thing' and this is what you did if you were a believer, but it was less an assurance and was more of a hope and "maybe He can" kind of thing.

But this time there was a difference in my attitude, and with each step I took, it was with an assurance and steadfast belief that God heals. I walked forward with an expectant heart; I believed that He would meet my need.

The same determination and steadfast belief as the woman with the issue of blood had when she battled through the crowds to touch the hem of Jesus' cloak. The same determination and steadfast belief of the friends of the man on the stretcher who made a way through the roof of the house to lower the man on the stretcher to Jesus. I don't think for one minute that these people thought "perhaps Jesus can heal us", or "we hope He can".

Well for the first time I truly experienced this steadfast belief not only for myself but now for others.

Roy stood with each person in turn not offering fancy, fluffy, long winded prayers but with a confidence and steadfast belief in healing. Roy did not promote his ministry with a load of theological nonsense and typical Irish blarney, but simply said 'what was on the box' - God heals, He meets our need, His love is unwavering.

The fact that God had seen me through my journey and battle enabled me to give everything to Him that night. While Roy stood with me, praying, I prayed with all my heart, with all the wonders of His amazing power, I stood before him with an open and vulnerable heart surrendering myself to Him.

There was no flash of lightening or a loud clash of thunder to signal a miracle had taken place. But I felt such a sense of hope and such a sense of expectation and warmth. As Roy continued to pray for others my expectant heart and steadfast prayers continued with the words of belief for both myself and others.

As I continued to stand in the moment and my peace, I became aware of a feeling that had started to slowly creep into my mouth. It felt as though I had bit into something tangy or sharp to taste. The corners of my mouth let out a twang, and a pulsating throb began on both sides of my face which had my ears ringing and warm. I was aware that my mouth was becoming very wet, my tongue was bathing in a wash of saliva. My swallowing reflex was enjoying normality. This was an experience I had forgotten.

The more I prayed and agreed with the prayers being offered for others around me the more my mouth bathed in the glory of His healing power.

The next day I was like Spit the Dog so delighted with my ability to spit and swallow. I was running around the church inviting everyone to peer into my mouth so that they could see all the moisture inside, and it is funny now to think that the ability to spit, normally seen as such an anti-social kind of thing was the cause of much rejoicing!

From that night onwards I have never had to sip water through the night, although I did need to remind my body and mind that I didn't need the regular ten mile trek to the toilet. The infections in my mouth have ceased since that day which is proof that the saliva glands are doing their job.

The Portrait of His Love

I guess that now I am writing my final chapter, I am thinking about the reasons that I decided to write this book in the first place. I am thinking about the way I felt back then, and the fact that I had originally thought I would write a little "testimony" – a little story of hope to share with my church friends!

My intentions had been simply to encourage them in their faith. After all, they had stood with me with thoughts and prayers and kind words, and I wanted them to know that it had all counted and made a difference.

However it has become very clear that the more I began to write, the more it became a journey in itself, a journey back through time, even right back to the beginning – somewhere I never thought I needed to go!

And going back I have realised that all of us who travel this road of life are constantly being shaped by events and situations, and are being taught lessons all the time – but do we really notice, or see, or learn?

One of the biggest things I guess my story proves is that any of us, regardless of faith, background, gender, whatever can find ourselves in situations that we have no control over. We all face times when we are thrown on the mercy of Fate, life, God, whatever you want to call it and are not able to help ourselves. In these times, we are made totally dependent on others. And this can be the most frightening thing of all, because for most of us, it is an alien situation to be in. It does not have to be a health matter; it can be any situation we find ourselves in where we are out of our depth and out of control.

For a person like me, this was especially terrifying. I had been stripped of everything that made me the woman I was, and in looking back I can see how this place made me really have to start to discover myself again, the real Susan, warts and all.

Writing this book has made me see how much I have changed, and how much I have learned, about myself and others and by sharing my story I have been able to really understand what the journey was all about. But it has also raised some questions for me that still remain unanswered.

I began my journey, on that blue settee, with very little faith. Oh yes I had a small faith in God that had him confined to the four walls of the church, but the notion of him being able to step into my reality, my real life – work, home, family life etc - was way beyond where I was at.

After all I was a very practical, down to earth woman who tended to only need God in the background because everything I had going on in my life was down to my carefully controlled and structured way of living. There had been a time in my past where God had had a greater impact on my life, but through the breakdown of my marriage and subsequent divorce, becoming independent and not being vulnerable again, not allowing myself to trust in anything or anyone but myself had become highly important to me. This was precisely where I was at when my journey began.

However, small though my faith was, in the back of my mind, there were still memories of a time when I had believed wholeheartedly. And though there was very little trust, I was not completely without an understanding of God.

This raises the question then, what if I had absolutely no idea of God? What if He had never been a figure in my life or history? Would he have still shown up in my story? Would I have been able to recognise him if he had?

I believe that it is not so much about faith or belief or understanding or trust that enables God to show up. It is something far more simple. It is the frightened desperate cry of a child that causes Father God to respond. When we have no hope or control, and we are left with nobody to hear our cry or the see the fear in our hearts – all we can do is cry out into the nothingness and just hope that someone hears us. And I now KNOW that he will turn up. What I only hoped for before, I now know without doubt!

But here's the question, because as we all know, Susan likes to ask the questions and get her answers. What if I had chosen not to believe, to shut the door on the possibility that God could show up for me? What if I had allowed age old bitterness and hurts to prevent me from even crying out to him? What if I had turned away the offers of prayer from my friends? What if I had shut my ears to the words of encouragement that some of them shared with me? What would my life have been like then?

Would I have felt more in control or less? Would the fears have been calmed or made worse? How would I have handled the breakdown in relationships and the disappointments that came with them? What sort of hope would I have clung to? When the darkness came whose voice would have reassured me? Where would my strength have come from?

Some people I realise have an amazing inner strength and are able to enter into the survival mode. This powerful force cannot be denied. It is a medical fact that positive thinking makes a massive difference in the healing process. And I know of many people who have beaten cancer with the strength that is already in them.

What difference therefore did my openness to God make to me?

The change in me is not just a physical one, or a spiritual one. Yes I am closer to God, and my body is healed of all traces of cancer, and yes there have been tiny miracles, the saliva returning to my mouth, the infection in my lymph nodes that just vanished, but the changes that have been most profound have been the ones that would never have occurred without the goodness of God in my life.

The bitterness that was shaping my life before the cancer came, no longer figures in my thinking, my feelings or my actions. I know that sometimes in times of trial and hardship people decide to let go of things that are petty and hurtful, because they have to concentrate on surviving, but once the period of survival is over, natural character emerges and when normality returns, so do normal thought patterns and behaviour.

But my natural patterns have been as comprehensively removed from my system as the cancer cells and my natural responses, the responses that were there before the blue settee day, are no longer my natural responses.

I think one of the most enduring lessons that I have learned, and one of the biggest changes of thought for me, is the fact that in certain situations it is quite okay if your belief in God is virtually non-existent or, as Jesus said, "small as a mustard seed". All that you need is a willingness to allow those people in your life who are offering you the life line of prayer, and their own faith in God and commitment to praying for you and standing in the gap for you, to do just that. After all what's the worst that can happen?

Obviously in my case, the worst that could happen would be the end of my life. But the best thing that could happen was a completely restored life - physically, emotionally, relationally and spiritually. In other words complete wholeness. I may not have had the faith for that myself, but I am glad that I allowed others to have that faith for me. Because now I can see what it was worth.

As I have said before, God had his own picture to paint of my life. Now that my story of this particular journey is over, I can really see the painting in full focus, and the beauty of it. I am seeing it now in the light as opposed to trying to work it out in the dark. The picture that I had been looking at in the dark had been colourless, without depth or true detail, but now, in the light, I can see shades, shapes, textures, vibrant colours, and subtle hues - all which completes the work of a perfect Artist, who over the last year has been creating something to share with everyone.

In walking with me on this journey, and now as we stand together, in these final steps checking out those finer details of the full picture, the high moments and the low, the dark nights and the bright days - I trust that you will not only have smiled at the funny moments, whilst perhaps feeling some of my pain, or wincing at some of the more yucky stuff, that you will have also come to a place of reassurance that no matter what we go through, and whatever questions and doubts we have, however we feel or fear that if we call out to God, he will always show up.

We may not recognise him straight away, we may not always be fully conscious of him but he always shows up in so many different ways.

For me he showed up in the soft song of a nurse, in the laughter of women on the ward, in the quiet light through a window, in the beauty of a tiny bird and then even in my final moments of resignation to the feeling that I was not going to make it, even then, he showed up in the words of a text from a friend.

Perhaps you have not, until reading this book, been aware of the many times God has shown up in your life. But as you have read this you have been reminded of similar incidents when you have "just known" that you were not alone, that someone was with you giving you strength. Perhaps now you realise that the "someone" was the person you don't really, in the cold light of day, believe in.

As I leave you now with that small thought, I would also like to say how much I appreciate that you have taken time to read my story. It has been a huge privilege to share my journey with you and I pray that it will make a difference to the way you now view and live your life.

Susan x

My Deepest Appreciation to...

My special, gentle, kind and loving husband and best friend Ron. We cried together and laughed together throughout the many challenges and fears of my journey. You cared for me during my darkest times and believed in our future life together. You were truly sent from God.

Kelly and Paula, my amazing daughters, my son-in-laws Adrian and John, and my grandchildren; I am extremely proud of you all. Your love and support gave me the strength to live when living was hard; your prayers helped me believe when believing was difficult. I am so very blessed to have such an amazing family.

Mum, Pete and sisters Hannah, Avril, Penny and families, despite the tragic journey you were all on you still found time to care for me, love me and call me your own. You made my wedding day so special when your hearts must have been breaking. I love you all.

.teve and Gladys, your prayers, belief and encourage-
.tent really made a difference during my battle and while
writing my story. You have both left an amazing footprint
in my life. Enjoy your heavenly party and save me a straw-
berry dipped in chocolate.

Dad and Carole, your determination and strength to
get me well never faltered. Spending hours driving me to
the hospital, sitting by my bedside and fighting your way
through a wall of fear was a wonderful gift from a father
and mother to a child. Our journey was a difficult one but
love can conquer all. I love you both.

Ron's sister Maria, brother-in-law Doug and family,
you were a much needed support for us both through our
journey. The love and belief you had in us and our future
together was amazing. You are a wonderful family and I am
proud to be part of it.

My amazing and wonderful friends, far too many to
name, I am very humbled by the support, love and time
you gave to show me how much you cared. Even through
the toughest times you prayed for me and believed I would
get better. True and faithful friends are a gift from God and
I thank Him for each one of you.

Liz, we have laughed and cried together as friends
throughout the years, and especially through the writing of
my story. Your gentleness and encouragement helped me
to continue to write when at times I struggled. You are
an inspiration. Friends reading this book will be eternally

grateful for your amazing gift in knowing where full stops and commas should be, allowing everyone to breath.

And finally, to my heavenly Father who lifted me up and held me close during the darkest nights and my most frightening times. You showed me unfailing love and gave me hope when I felt lost and lonely. You restored my life and made it new. You moulded me into a woman who has found the freedom to be vulnerable, to trust and to believe in your promises. I truly dared to believe.

If you would like further information or support with any-thing you have read, then please contact Now Church on 01909 732731 or via our website www.nowchurch.org.uk or email un info@nowchurch.org.uk We'd love to hear from you.

Twitter: @susanybarnett

21262504R00137

Made in the USA
Charleston, SC
11 August 2013